The man who can fling a craving on you,
JERRY CLOWER,
lets it all out in the exuberant story of his life.

"I'm the product of a broken home, but I want to hasten to say that the Lord Jesus Christ can mend a broken home and make it stronger after the break than it was before. . . .

"I don't care how good you can pick a guitar, how good you can sing, how good you can tell a story, how good you can perform . . . if you still ain't good people, you ain't nothing. . . .

"I want America to be one great big country, and everybody's Americans, and everybody's loving one another and getting it on. . . .

"God ain't gonna put no more on you than you can stand. . . .

"Never underestimate the power of Satan. There is a devil, he is real, and he does go around like a roaring lion trying to devour folks. . . .

"I've turned all my hang-ups over to the one what was hung up for my hang-ups."

AIN'T GOD GOOD!

by

JERRY CLOWER
with GERRY WOOD

PUBLISHED BY POCKET BOOKS NEW YORK

AIN'T GOD GOOD!

Word Books edition published 1975

POCKET BOOK edition published January, 1977

This POCKET BOOK edition includes every word contained in
the original, higher-priced edition. It is printed from brand-
new plates made from completely reset, clear, easy-to-read type.
POCKET BOOK editions are published by
POCKET BOOKS,
a division of Simon & Schuster, Inc.,
A GULF+WESTERN COMPANY
630 Fifth Avenue,
New York, N.Y. 10020.
Trademarks registered in the United States
and other countries.

Contents

Photographs appear at the center of the book.

Jerry's Preface

FOR THE PAST several years as I have attended functions of my church and as I have witnessed for Christ in my everyday vocation, several of my friends and my pastor have suggested that I put some of my experiences down in writing.

I prayed about this, and it got to where after speaking to a Cattlemen's meeting or a fertilizer conference someone would come up to me and say, "You should put some of these experiences in writing." I never felt led to do it.

One day after speaking at a dairy convention in South Alabama, a guy came up to me and said, "Why don't you put some of your experiences on record?" I did, and it has been successful. After having done five long-playing albums and all of them hits, people keep saying, "Jerry, you ought to write a book."

Well now I feel led that I ought to write a book. After praying and meditating over this, I feel convicted to put some of this down. It has been done. It is done with the prayer that it'll help others to laugh as they walk as Christian disciples in their everyday lives.

I think everybody ought to be a laughing Christian. I'm convinced that there's just one place where there's not any laughter, and that's hell. I've made arrangements to miss hell. So ha-ha-ha! and hallelujah! I ain't never going to have to be nowhere where some folks ain't laughing. If you're walking around with a hump in your back and your lips pooched out and you don't believe in laughing, then you ought to go home and look in the mirror and see what all us other folks been *laughing* at for all these many years.

Speaking from my heart, I'd like to say to my family, I can never express my deep appreciation. There's just no way. And I'd like to express my undying gratitude to so many of my co-workers in show business, my manager—Tandy Rice—members of my family, friends, and folks I've known through the years who have encouraged me and prayed for me in everything that I've done.

Finally I dedicate this book to my childhood sweetheart—a young lady with whom I had the blessing of making a public profession of my faith in Christ, the lady who is now the mother of my four children. And I some kind of love her. So to her I dedicate this book and affectionately say, "This book is dedicated to that woman what lives with Mr. Clower."

Gerry's Preface

To Jerry from Gerry
. . . with love

WELL, JERRY, I'M on the Panama Limited heading home from your home. And, riding this train, I recall your explanation of why the town of Magnolia, Mississippi—a few miles back down the line—calls itself America's Cleanest City: "The Panama Limited comes through there twice a day doing a hundred miles an hour, and it just sucks everything off the street—scheewooo!—when she comes through." I asked my porter if that were true, and he replied, "No, sir. We just go seventy-nine miles an hour through there." But a railroad man named John Henry McGehee told me that, sure enough, he took his trains through Magnolia at a full-throttle one hundred.

Your stories, like you, are larger than life, giving us the opportunity to observe human nature without a microscope or telescope. Naked truth for naked eyes.

9

And now I know why you're so strong, so energetic, so *good*. It's the people and the earth you come from.

First I met your mother—and what a lady that lady is! She spread a luncheon table with more food on it than anything I've seen outside Thanksgiving. When I left five hours later and she gave me a hug and kiss, I felt like I'd known her since I was a baby.

Love, Jerry, that's what it is.

And I met your stepdad who is more of a father to you than many real fathers are to their blood sons. I might have used the wrong word there, Jerry, because he is *really* your father and you are *really* his son. Love makes it that way.

Your brother Sonny is a Clower all right. And he can tell some pretty funny stories, too. Like that man at the football game who was toting about twenty hotdogs and a dozen Cokes but couldn't find the people he was sitting with. So he gave his hot dogs to y'all and sat with you, too, while his hungry/thirsty friends in that crowded stadium wondered where in the world he went to get that food.

I noticed that you never refer to your brother as "Sonny." It's always, *"My brother* Sonny." Pride, love, and admiration merge into each word.

Sonny's wife, Jody, prepared me for what Homerline was like. You Clower boys really know how to marry above yourselves, don't you?

Homerline. Now when a man talks about his woman as much as you talk about Homerline, something is very wrong or very right. And this is very right. One look at her smile and I knew why you are so wild about her.

Jesus smiles on this family.

The cycle of love continues in those beautiful children—Ray off at college, Amy off at marriage, Sue blooming in the sensitivity and innocence of her early teens, and that perky little Katy, a handful of years old. She told me about her friend that nobody else can see. Malcolm Abercut Dinko is his name. "Where is he now?" I asked. Katy muffled a giggle with one hand and pointed to my hair with the other. "He's sitting on top of your head!" Before I left, she slipped me some candy so I wouldn't get hungry on the train. I didn't have the heart to tell her there was a dining car on board.

Then I met your next-door neighbor, Chief Hill— an artist with a welding torch and an artist at living. I expected grits and gravy in the Deep South, but kibbie and mischee? Marguerite Hill had been fixing it since sunrise. Oh, was that something! And there was Chief Hill's answer when I asked him if it were possible to weld a crack in my Franklin fireplace: "I can weld everything except a broken heart and the break of day."

Off to your church to hear Brother Yates tell us that every time we see a police car or a lock on a door it's a reminder of the sin in our society.

We traveled the highways through the hamlets and drove down the back roads of old Mississippi lush with blood-darkened soil and infinite greenery that looked like my old Kentucky homeland. Which reminds me to dedicate my efforts in this book to my parents now seeking to sift a little gold from their golden years, my wife who knows how to handle a husband prone to spend twenty-eight consecutive hours behind a typewriter, my grandparents who have died but live in me, and the wonderful friends I share life and love with.

Your stories came alive again as I saw where Marcel did the deed with the chain saw. A new beer joint stood on the site. The old one either burned, rotted, or Marcel did more cutting than you let on (though I've never known you to undertell a story). I saw where John Eubanks treed the Supercoon and needed some relief, and where Uncle Virsi Ledbetter got spilled from his wheelchair in the swamp one night and beat everybody and the dogs back to the house.

Through your talent, the soul of the Southland opened itself to me and welcomed me onto the soil of this lovely land of tragedy, contradiction, and compassion that we both love so much. Lord, how Mark Twain and Will Rogers and William Faulkner would have loved you and your stories.

Yazoo City is one exuberant name for a town in sleepy Mississippi, and somehow that exuberance has rubbed off on your Rt. 4 life-style and personality. You're big enough for two and a half football players and a waterboy thrown in.

You're energy, enthusiasm . . . every man who has ever wanted to follow his dream. You're father, brother, and lover of life, a Southern gentleman, an American, and a citizen of the world, dedicated to fun and fundamentalism.

With a heart that belongs to the century and a soul that belongs to Jesus, it's a pleasure to call you friend, friend.

Just as every hello is only a prelude to good-by and every spring spawns its fall, my trip to your heartland was too soon over. With a little boy zeal, you checked your watch and yelled, "On time!" as my train highballed into McComb. You looked wistfully at the Panama Limited gleaming and hissing proud in the night and declared, "I wish I could catch the train with you and go all the way to Chicago. We'd get us a room on there and go to the diner and . . ."

Then you told me to be sure to try the roast beef dinner, and when I hopped aboard, the Limited left so fast that I recalled your story of how Marcel Ledbetter boarded this same train in McComb bound for New Orleans, stopped on the bottom step, turned around to kiss his mama good-by, and kissed a bull in the mouth at Hammond, Louisiana.

All I can say, Jerry, is that y'all are some kind of people living some kind of life.

Peace, Godlove, and happiness to all of you all of the time.

Love,
GERRY

P.S. I didn't mean to eat so much lunch at your mother's house, but that food was great! You said what

Tandy Rice did to the fried okra (ate the whole bowl) I did to everything on the table. That's true, Jerry, but just remember that the only things on the table were homemade cornpone, biscuits, butter, molasses, preserves, turnips with hot pepper sauce, sweet potatoes, lima beans, rice, onions, chicken and dumplings, fruitcake, peaches with whipped cream and syrup, poundcake, iced tea, and coffee. By the time we got through, it was almost time for supper.

I know I had several helpings of everything, but the biggest helping I had was of Love. And I'll never forget it.

1

How It All Happened

BACK AT THE beginning of the '20s people moved into this long-leaf pine country, set up huge sawmills, and cut the timber. Thousands and thousands of feet of beautiful pine timber were cut right here. The mounds where sawdust accumulated are now covered up, and grass grows over them.

My grandfather, old man Eugene Clower, was a saw-filer. He was following this sawmill filing saws. His son Otha—everybody called him Buster—drove a truck for Graves's Mill, and old man Tobe Graves was married to my daddy's aunt. He was kind of in the family. And this young Buster Clower drove a truck.

The most humble man I've ever known in my life —Mr. Wesley Burns—died a pauper because he gave away everything he had. He was married to Aunt Kate Burns—that's why my little girl is named Katy. Katy and Wesley Burns had a daughter named Mable. She married Buster Clower the truck driver. And Buster and Mable lived in one of the houses across the gravel road in front of the sawmill.

September 28, 1926, Howard Gerald Clower was born. They nicknamed him Jerry. Dr. Hart from McComb, Mississippi, delivered him. Dr. Howard Gerald, a doctor over at East Fork Community, was going to deliver Jerry Clower, but he died just before Jerry was born. So they named me after Dr. Howard Gerald.

Across the road from Graves's Mill, Rt. 4, Liberty, Mississippi, is where it all happened. It was just a regular shotgun house. People who worked at the sawmill lived there—the quarters.

My brother Sonny is eighteen months older than I am. My father heard the depression was coming on and that there were some jobs in Memphis, Tennessee, in the railroad shops. When I was three weeks of age, my daddy caught the train at McComb, Mississippi, and went to Memphis and got a big job in the railroad shops. That's where he got into a fraternal order and learned how to drink and ended up an alcoholic.

Other sins followed the addiction of drinking, and my mother had to get out. My mother, my brother Sonny, and little Jerry returned to Amite County, Mississippi, the place of our birth. We went back to Rt. 4, Liberty, Mississippi, and moved in with my grandpa.

This is when I started digging my living out of a little forty-acre farm. I've climbed every tree and walked all the way through the woods to my house.

I have walked down this hill toting a cotton sack with my brother Sonny and my mother. She'd pick two rows of cotton, and me and my little old brother would pick one and try to keep up. I've seen the blood oozing out from under her fingernails, picking that cotton, those cottonburrs sticking her . . . a beautiful woman. She isn't a bad-looking woman now.

She'd quit about 11:30 and go to the house and whip up a little hoecake meal, and we'd go up there and sop molasses with that bread and go back down there and work. We worked like dogs and didn't have anything—we were poor. Mother got a job with the WPA helping a recreational director with a program in the county. She had an old A-model car that she drove to Liberty to work. We survived with that.

One day a carload of Southwest Junior College students came out here "gal-ing"—coming out into the country and dating girls. One fellow was named Elliott Moore, one was named Red McDaniel, and another was named Stinky Edwards. Elliott Moore dated my mother. This went on for a while. One day in 1939 they told us, "We're going to Jackson and get Dr. Hewitt at the First Baptist Church, a native Amite Countian, to marry us."

Elliott Moore was a plasterer. He worked with his hands and had arms like a nail keg. He'd get up on a scaffold and take those plastering tools and smear that mud on there. He'd leave and go to a job in Natchez or McComb, even Baton Rouge. He went to a bank in Magnolia, Mississippi, borrowed sixteen hundred dollars, and bought a house and two hundred acres. It'd sell for a quarter-million now.

Me and my mother and Sonny left my granddaddy's house, moved up the gravel road, and moved in with our new stepfather, Elliott Moore. When he went off to plaster, he'd leave a list of jobs he wanted us to do. He was pretty firm. He thought you ought to give an honest day's work for an honest day's pay. He thought if you tell a young'un to cut his hair, he ought to cut his hair. Every Sunday morning when we'd get up, it was automatic—we knew we were going to church.

This is where I was raised. That old tin building was the milk shed—I had to do the milking. That's the same old barn. My brother fed the mules. We waited for the school bus right there by the mail box. I sat on that bank a million times waiting for the Sears and Roebuck mail order to come. I had me some new shoes ordered. When they wouldn't come, I'd cry. We had a great big old bulldog named Mike that helped raise us. If mother wanted to whip one of us, she had to shut him up in the milk barn. He'd bite her if she hit us.

That's when things began to pick up. We didn't have an awful lot of money or modern conveniences. We still had a two-hole outdoor privy, and we drew water out of the reservoir to take a bath. Elliott Moore was our stepfather, and we were the Clower boys, and he had some mules, and we plowed and made crops and farmed. Sonny and I would make the crops. Elliott Moore would supervise, and we'd have a wage hand or two. I plowed a mule all over this country. This is a shed we built years ago. He keeps scaffold boards under it now. That's a catfish pond—he's got a lot of catfish in there.

We had a pond way over there on the hill that we went to. Redwing blackbirds roosted in there, the most beautiful things you ever saw. We caught the school bus every morning. The sides were open where you normally would have a window. The old bus had a canvas on it, and on cold days you rolled down the canvas and tied it as best you could. Later on we got a bus with windows in it. Every evening we'd get off and walk up to the house, change into our overalls, and pick cotton or whatever there was to do.

One day one of the guys on the bus hollered, "Get that cotton sack and go to that field!" and I said, "I ain't gonna pick no cotton today." My daddy, Elliot Moore—we called him Babe—said, "Go get your sack."

"Babe, you said we weren't going to pick cotton today."

"Yeah, but I need to teach you that you don't ever say what you ain't going to do. Because you may have to do something that you ain't planning on doing. So don't ever pop off about what you won't do because you may have to do it. So go get your sack. I think it'd do you good to pick this evening."

One day Babe had me and Sonny and a black fellow named Sam Holmes clearing trees out, and we heard a hollering and a whooping and some people having a good time down at the swimming hole. Since Babe wasn't around, I dropped my overalls—that's all I had on anyhow—and said, "Let's go swimming." I cut right across the road, left the bank atop a cliff, and jumped—about twenty feet down—and hollered,

"Waaayaahhhh!" like Tarzan, with spraddled-out legs. Halfway down, I looked—and there was a bunch of ladies looking at me. I didn't stop in midair, but I tried to. I hit the water, went under, swam way over to some bushes, flew out of the water, and kept running.

In school, I liked any course you could read and remember like civics or literature, but I despised anything where you had to diagram a sentence or figure out mathematics. I can remember right now in the literature book as you turn toward the back in this green book, here in the upper left-hand corner: William Shakespeare was born in 1564 and died in 1616. Born at Stratford-on-Avon, England. Wrote during the Elizabethan period. Some of his tragedies were *Macbeth* and *Julius Caesar*. He wrote *As You Like It*. I can still see that. I made a hundred on anything I could remember. I was a B student. If I had studied and applied myself, I could have been an A student. But I enjoy talking and nosing around.

Living near us was a man who ran a shop and gristmill. He raised his children on a dirt floor. He was an alcoholic. Some of the things he did were comical, but as I look back on it now, it was pitiful.

To show you how great this country is, every one of his children amounted to something—got fine jobs, married. One of them is the head shop foreman in one of the biggest car dealerships in the South. He inherited his daddy's knowledge about mechanics.

Let this be a lesson to the world. My daddy-in-law, Mr. Homer Wells, was one of the most godly men I've ever known in my life. A man who lived over yonder once told me, "If I wanted a neighbor, I would get God to make a man like Homer Wells. He's the finest neighbor I ever had."

He was so beautiful that he wouldn't say anything bad about anybody. Some of us boys actually tried to trick him on several occasions by saying something about somebody that wasn't good. So when the man

who lived nearby got killed, I went to the funeral. Pa
Homer was there, and there stood all of the man's
little children who had been raised on a dirt floor and
had been mistreated due to strong drink and whiskey.
I put my arm around Pa Homer and whispered, "Pa
Homer, isn't it awful that the fellow's dead? Look at
his children standing around his grave crying that he's
gone, and he never did anything for them. Wasn't he
sorry?"

Pa Homer looked up at me. "Jerry, if you didn't
want a favor done for you, you'd better not let that
fellow know you wanted it done. He was one of the
most accommodating men I've ever known in my life."
That's what he said at the man's burial. Homer Wells
—my daddy-in-law.

My brother Sonny and I went to the Baptist Young
People's Union over at East Fork Baptist Church. A
very wonderful lady named Eleanor Wells was the
leader of that group. Had I known that one day she
was going to be my mother-in-law, I wouldn't have
acted as ugly as I did as a young'un in that department.

We got in on Sunday night December 7, 1941, and
my mother met us on the front steps. "Boys, the
Japanese bombed Pearl Harbor."

"Where is it?" Sonny asked.

"It's out in the Pacific."

"Well, who does it belong to?"

"It belongs to the United States of America," I said.

"They ain't got no cause to bomb us."

And my brother kept pestering our mother until she
signed the papers for him to join the United States
Navy. He was a high-school dropout, seventeen years
of age, when he went into the navy as an apprentice
seaman. He was discharged a couple years ago as a
navy commander with sixteen battle stars. He was a
war hero, and most of it was in the submarine service.
He went through it all.

Sonny is an electronics genius. He worked college
calculus just as a hobby when we were in high school.

I don't know calculus. They told me in that algebra class to solve for X, and I finally figured out what X was. Then they said, "Now we want to know what Y is." And I'd give up. If X didn't suit them, I sure wasn't going to find out what Y was because I solved that X and I figured that was enough.

You judged who lived in East Fork by the church they went to. There's just one great big country church in this settlement. The folks who say, "I live out at East Fork," are primarily the ones who belong to the East Fork Baptist Church. The church was founded and built in 1810.

On the fourth Sunday every July, the East Fork Baptist Church has a revival meeting. They have been doing this since 1810. The day of the revival—the fourth Sunday in July, 1939—my mother cooked a chicken pie and some egg custards, and we came to church for the revival meeting. I sat in the church that Sunday, heard the singing and a sermon, then we all went outside to a big table between some sweetgum trees. We spread our dinner and ate. They called it dinner on the grounds. Then we came back into the church and sang. The choir would really be singing good—beautiful, old-timey hymns: "Amazing Grace," "When the Roll Is Called Up Yonder"—and the preacher would preach again.

Rev. Pardue from the First Baptist Church of Magnolia, Mississippi, was the visiting preacher. Coach C. C. "Hot" Moore, who coached the McComb football team, was the song leader. While sitting there that Sunday, I saw a little blond-headed girl in the churchhouse. I thought she was pretty and figured I'd work it around and see if I could hold her hymnbook. And I did.

They had services every morning and night of that week. Thursday night, I was sitting in church, and Brother Pardue got up in that pulpit and said, "For all have sinned and come short of the glory of God."

Well, he ain't talking about everybody, I thought.

"I'm talking about General Eisenhower, Franklin Delano Roosevelt, and Douglas MacArthur."

Now that was three of my heroes.

"The Bible says 'For *all* have sinned and come short of the glory of God."

Well, I got to listening to this.

"Also, continuing in the Book of Romans out of the Bible, "The wages of sin is death.' "

I said to myself, "My soul, if everybody's a sinner and the wages of sin is death, then I'm in a mess."

Rev. Pardue smiled. "But God commended his love toward us and while we were yet sinners, Christ died for us. And if you'll confess with your mouth to the Lord Jesus and believe in your heart that God raised him from the dead, you can be saved."

So while they were singing hymn 197, "Only Trust Him," I walked down the aisle and took my pastor, Rev. Price Brock, by the hand. And I had that experience of grace that only comes from the saving power of God. During that same night, there walked this little blonde whose book I had been holding. She too publicly professed her faith in Christ at the same time.

Amite River runs straight down, and it forks north of here. The west prong runs over the other side of Liberty; the east prong flows right by the church. This is the baptizing hole.

Everybody walked down from the church. The preacher and me and my Homerline—a little thirteen-year-old girl—walked into the shallow water waist deep. And the choir sang on the bank, "Yes, we'll gather at the river . . ." We were baptized together.

Since then they've put a baptistery in the church, but you'd be surprised, some folks still want to be baptized in the river—and they bring them down here. Me and my brother Sonny and my wife Homerline were baptized right there.

After I was converted, I went on to school here and finished high school in April, 1944. The next morning I joined the United States Navy. I had grieved myself near about to death because my only brother had left home for the navy. I was home by myself and could hardly stand it. He was going through training at Great Lakes, Illinois. Then he got on a submarine— and I wanted to get on a submarine so bad, I couldn't stand it. I wanted to be like my brother Sonny.

I joined the navy and was sent to Camp Perry at Williamsburg, Virginia. Then I went to the radio school at Miami University at Oxford, Ohio—and later caught the S.S. *Matsonian* out of San Francisco, went overseas in the navy, and was assigned to an aircraft carrier. On my nineteenth birthday I had already received the Presidential Unit Citation and three battle stars.

I got my discharge some thirty months later in New Orleans, caught the Panama Limited, got off it at McComb, and hitchhiked home. As I walked up on the front porch, my mama ran out and grabbed me and kissed me and said, "Baby, you and your brother Sonny were missing in action—both at the same time. It's been kind of rough. Now here you are safe and your brother Sonny is safe on a submarine in the South Pacific. We're so thankful. We've been praying for your safe return. Now what is it, son, you intend to do?"

"Mama, do you remember how me and my brother Sonny used to sit out on the front porch and listen to that battery radio, and that McComb, Mississippi, would be playing that football?"

Sonny and I would actually cry because we lived out in the county and didn't have an opportunity to go to a high school where they played football. We wanted to play so bad but couldn't. I finished high school with seven other folks. Well, McComb would be playing Laurel or Catholic High of Memphis, Meridian, or Biloxi, and we'd listen to it on the radio. Both of us thought we'd be good at it if we had the chance to try it.

"I'm going off to college. And I'm going to play football. I'm going to fulfill my life's ambition."

"But the closest you've ever come to playing football in your lifetime was kicking a Pet Milk can in the middle of the gravel road at East Fork School at recess. How in the world do you intend to go off and play?"

"I intend to do it. I'm going to play."

I wasn't fat in those days. I was six feet tall, 214 pounds, and had just turned twenty. I put on one of those tight-fitting navy T-shirts and sucked myself up where my physique would show real good. I went out to Southwest Mississippi Junior College at Summit. When I walked up on that campus, those folks got to looking at me. Directly, one of them walked up. "May I help you?"

"I'm looking for the football coach."

When those folks saw how I was strutting and how muscled up I was, they were trying to find the coach, too.

So I went with them into the office, and this coach jumped up. "Son, who are you?"

"I'm Jerry Clower from Rt. 4, Liberty, Mississippi, a graduate of East Fork Consolidated High School. I'm a football player, and I intend to enroll here next week."

"Son, I'll give you a half scholarship just looking at you. But tell me quick, what position do you play?"

"Sir, I believe I am the man what runs with the football. That's the position I play."

I went out for football, practiced sixteen days, and the first college football game I ever saw, I played in it. I played at Southwest Junior College for two years, and a friend at McComb wrote to Mississippi State and said he believed ol' Jerry Clower was worthy of a look-see. I went to Mississippi State because I wanted to major in agriculture, and I played up there.

I wanted to get a degree in agriculture and be a 4-H Club agent because of the impression Mr. Monroe McElveen made upon my life when I was a young boy in Amite County. I so respected him and the job he was doing as a 4-H Club agent that I wanted to grow up one day to be like him. That's about the finest compliment you can pay a man.

At Mississippi State they were good to me, patient

with me, and they let me play in the Southeastern Conference. One of my life's ambitions was to letter in college—and there I was playing in the SEC.

I believe I can refresh your memory to where you can remember when I played. Auburn University had a fine All-American running back by the name of Travis Tidwell. I am the man—the defensive tackle in 1949 before standing room only at the Auburn stadium— that Travis Tidwell picked up twenty-seven yards running backwards over. (Actually it was seven yards, but in running the seven yards, he made a first down, so that made it seventeen. So I just exaggerated ten more. It felt like 104 yards.)

After playing football, I'm a sports fanatic. I love football, keep up with it, even change my schedule to where I'll get to a place early enough to watch a game on television. I don't travel while they're going on if I can help it because about all the relaxation I really get is to sit and watch a football game on television. Then there'll be basketball. I keep up with it religiously, and I look forward to coming home from church, getting barefooted, having lunch, and watching a game.

I do a lot of sports awards banquets like the *Nashville Banner* Banquet of Champions. That one event probably had as much to do with launching my show business career as any performance I've ever done. There were so many heavyweight folks from the music industry there.

We gave Jerry a thousand-dollar check for his appearance, and he gave it back to us to give to a charity.

RED O'DONNELL
Nashville Banner

A great deal can be learned from sports, and I advocate that all young people participate in some type, especially football, if they can. It's one of the few things that a kid can excel in that his mama and papa can't buy him. You see the big debutante parties and all this stuff. Folks got money, and they buy that for their kids. Parents even shove their kids up the social ladder which sometimes is tragic because some of them don't want to be pushed up the ladder.

A kid doesn't have to start the game or be first string to excel. All he's got to do is the best he can with what he's got, even if most of the time he sits on the bench. I'd like for you to show me a good football team that just had eleven folks.

I was out in California not too long ago, did a show, then took a walk by the motel. There were fifty kids wearing leather jackets, racing the motors on their motorcycles. Waaaooooomm! Waaooooommm! All of them had on dark sunglasses, and it was twelve o'clock midnight. There wasn't a star in the sky, and it'd be hours before the sun would come up. I asked one of them, "What are y'all doing?"

"Man, we're getting attention. Folks are noticing us."

"If you got guts enough, you can go down to the local high school, and the football coach will issue you some gear, and if you want to show folks how tough you are, not only can you get attention, but thousands of people will turn out and pay money to get to see you. And they'll even play the band while you're showing everybody how tough you are."

It was General MacArthur who said if he had one crucial battle to fight, he'd want to fight it with athletes. There's a great lesson in winning and paying the price to achieve something. And some of the things we get now just come too easy.

During my year of football at Mississippi State, we tied one game. In that losing season I learned that you can catch more flies with sugar than you can with vinegar. We had a coach who felt like you could catch more flies with vinegar than with sugar. It was one of the real distasteful things of my life to see how a coach could treat grown adult men and think he could motivate them when he had just the opposite effect.

Your great coaches reasoned and bragged on folks. If you brag on me, I'll kill myself for you, but if you tell me how sorry I am or grab me in the collar and shake me and cuss me, that ain't the way to do it.

2

The Woman What Lives
with Mr. Clower

I've always been able to talk things through with
Jerry. As far as arguments—that's something
neither one of us has done. Neither one of us likes
an argument anyway. So why argue?

Jerry has always been real thoughtful in that I
always know exactly when he's coming in. If not,
he calls. He's a minuteman, too. If he says he's
going to be here at five o'clock, he'll be here at
five o'clock.

HOMERLINE CLOWER

HOMERLINE WELLS AND I had started courting. Even
when I was off in the service, I never really dated
another girl with any seriousness at all. Homerline is
the only girl I've ever really cared for. Today she's
the mother of my four children, and I some kind of
love her. We have a Christian home where love is.

If God gave me the ingredients and told me to make
a woman, I'd make her exactly like my wife. I don't
know of a thing I'd change about her. I know people

will say, "Well, you *know* he's crazy," but I've got to be honest about this. I'm simply recommending to young people that God said it would work. And it will work. After becoming Christians, me and mama have used the Bible as a guide to try to get it on like the Lord said. I don't know of any better way to do it.

One summer during college vacation, I got a job with a contractor building the new East Fork grammar school. I quit work one Friday evening, got up the next morning, drove to Hattiesburg, Mississippi, picked up Homerline at the University of Southern Mississippi, drove back to the old East Fork house, dressed, drove over to East Fork Baptist Church, and was married, August 15, 1947.

Me and Homerline have got it on. We've never had a fuss. Ask our kids. If we disagree, we sit down and talk about it. I hesitate to say this publicly because people think you're lying. I've never raised my voice to my wife in my life, and she's never raised her voice at me. When the Bible says you become as one flesh, we literally are.

In Jonesboro, Arkansas, a tornado killed forty people. I helped drag the bodies out of that water. When the water went down, I got in my car and drove home. The next morning I came in at eight o'clock. When I stepped in the kitchen, Homerline threw her towel down, ran, grabbed me, and said, "Oh, darling, what's the matter? What's wrong?"

"What do you mean 'what's wrong?' "

"What's wrong?"

Then I told her. She knew I had been through some kind of ordeal, and I hadn't opened my mouth.

There's not enough of that in the world. That's what we need. To get it on. Compassion.

Sometimes I get to thinking that I'm *something*. The man on the radio called me the greatest humorist in America. I'm a *hoss*. I'll speak to the church some morning, and I'll fling a craving on them. While we're driving home, Homerline will put her hand on my leg and say, "Honey, you got kind of wound up this morning, didn't you?"

No matter how great I think I am, she can usually come up with somebody who's greater.

One day a bunch of women in town went to get the high-school football coach fired because he had cussed in front of their children. They said he called them chicken-blank. Homerline went to the meeting and said, "I was trying to think of what word would describe the way they played the other night, and that's the word." Well, it broke up the meeting.

My wife loves me every day. One of the things that shows how we love one another: I may not be home for her birthday or we might not be together for mine, but when we see one another we say, "Did you have a happy birthday?" We might not give one another anything. Every day's a birthday with us. Our anniversary is the same way. Every day is our anniversary.

One of the greatest expressions of love that my wife ever exhibited to me was when my Sue was born. We were at the King's Daughters Hospital in Yazoo City. This was our third child. My wife never wants to go to the hospital until it's time. We almost waited too late. We got over there, and thirty minutes later, Sue was born. I'm standing at the swinging doors outside the delivery room. As the doors swung open at 6:30 P.M. and they rolled out the stretcher table that my wife was on after giving birth to Sue just a few minutes before, I looked down and said, "Honey, we got us a little cheerleader." She raised her tired eyes toward me and asked, "Honey, have you had any supper?"

What was I to do? Grab her and say, "No! There's no excuse for you not to have the table set. Get up from there, woman! You ought to be cooking me a pot of peas. All you've done is just gone in there and had a young'un."

Having my baby was some kind of loving me. But worrying about *me* while she was having one . . . oh, what a woman.

3

Fathers

I'M THE PRODUCT of a broken home. My mama and daddy separated when I was a little boy, and ultimately they divorced.

I've never before said anything about my daddy. But I am now.

Even though I'm the product of a broken home, under the proper circumstances the break can be mended, and it'll be stronger than it ever was before it was ever broken. This is the Christian connotation of a Christian home. We didn't have a Christian home. My mama remarried, and then we did. My stepfather is closer to me than if he were my blood daddy. That made all the difference in the world.

My brother and I have sat in the third grade at East Fork Consolidated School all alone while Cherokee Bill was putting on a little show in the main auditorium, and it cost a nickel to go see it. They announced the day before, "Bring your nickel." But we didn't have one, so we didn't see it. But from the time my mama married my stepfather up to this second, I've never needed a nickel that I couldn't go get one from him. I had me a daddy what had me a nickel then. And it makes a lot of difference.

Every child, every young man, ought to have the right to stand flatfooted and say, "My papa was a godly man, my papa was a fellow I could go to with my problems." Unfortunately, this wasn't so.

I got a fan letter the other day. I saw a letter in this big stack of mail that had my return address on it. I slipped it out, and it was addressed to me in the handwriting of a child. I opened it up.

Dear Mother and Daddy. Thank you for being such fine Christian parents. You show me how I ought to act. Love, Sue.

That was from my twelve-year-old daughter. I was thrilled to death, and I praised God for getting such a letter. Then after I stood there and thought about it a while, I was indeed sad thinking about the untold thousands of young girls who cannot write that kind of letter.

One reason I'm a teetotaler is that I got so disgusted being mistreated due to a man's drinking excess that I never have wanted to run the risk of mistreating my own family by drinking. People give me a lot of credit for not drinking, but I don't deserve it.

When I was a little bitty boy, my mother, my brother Sonny, and I left Memphis where my daddy was working. The drink problem got so rough that we got out and went to Big Daddy's at Rt. 4, Liberty, Mississippi.

My father kept writing, "I've turned over a new leaf. If you'll come back and bring my two boys, I'll promise you I'll never drink again." He worked for the railroad and sent us a pass, so we caught the train at McComb and went back to Memphis. We got off the train—me, Sonny, and my mother who is eighteen years older than I am and just kind of a teenager, if you please.

My daddy met us, and he was drunk. We were

scared to death. He actually could hardly find the apartment where we were supposed to live. There we were without money, back up there in that mess, and didn't know what in the world to do. No way to get back out of it because we didn't have any money. We couldn't say, "Give us a pass, we're leaving again." We couldn't do that. I don't know how my mother arranged it, but we finally got back out of it, and ultimately the divorce did follow. We went back to Rt. 4, Liberty, the place of my birth, and that's where we stayed. We never did go back any more.

My mother, wanting to be fair and to give him every chance in the world, had gone back, and he had met us at the train drunk. Now here's a parallel to that.

I promised my children back in March, 1955, that I would take them on a little trip while they had a holiday from school. I was coming home for the holiday to be with my family, and we were going to see Big Daddy and Big Mama. I was in Jonesboro, Arkansas, selling stock in a new expansion of Mississippi Chemical Corporation, and I got tied up with some big prospects. There was no way I could get home because I had some appointments the next morning. I called my wife and told her. Homerline said, "Honey, the kids are going to be so disappointed because Ray and Amy are here. They're just waiting for you to drive up any minute, knowing they're going to get to travel with you these next two days."

"Honey, I cannot get home, but I'll tell you what. How about putting them on the *City of New Orleans?* It leaves Canton, Mississippi, at eleven in the morning and gets to Memphis the middle of the afternoon. I'll drive from Jonesboro over to Memphis, and I'll meet them, bring them back, and put them in the motel here at Jonesboro. We'll stay together these two days, and they can travel with me up in the foothills of Missouri, and we'll have a good time."

"That's fine. They'll get a train ride, too."

My wife put Ray and Amy on the train, and I went to the Memphis depot to meet them. And all of a sudden it dawned on me that a few years before my own father stood exactly in the same place where I stood.

I remembered coming here . . . ooh, I remembered that. I had been on the train with my brother Sonny —the same age of Ray and Amy—when we were coming to Memphis to see my daddy. Now here was the thing again, several years later. Here's my children coming to Memphis to see *their* daddy.

And tears started running down my cheeks. Under my breath, I'm saying, "Praise God, hallelujah! my kids are coming to see their daddy, and when they get off that train, their daddy's going to be cold sober and going to love them, and we're going to have a good time." I started thanking the Lord that my kids and my situation was now diametrically reversed to the situation that I saw years before.

Ray and Amy got off the train, and the black porter was smiling from ear to ear. He had Ray by one hand and Amy by the other. I walked up and they shouted, "There's my daddy!" I got down on one knee, and they ran and grabbed me.

The porter said, "Sir, you'll have to show some identification. I know these children say you're their daddy, but the Illinois Central Railroad . . ." And this impressed me very much. I showed him a driver's license, and he said, "If your name is Clower, you can have these two lovely children. We've enjoyed having them on our railroad."

Ray and Amy bragged on the black man being nice to them all the way up from Mississippi. As we were walking through the depot, Ray said, "Daddy, you see that lady walking over yonder?"

"Yeah."

"She's a Christian and a Baptist."

"Son, how do you know?"

"Well, me and Amy was singing on the train coming up."

"Singing?"

"Yes, sir. We were singing 'Power in the Blood'—

one of them old hymns. The lady came walking up to us and said, 'You children sound like y'all are Baptists.' We said, 'Well, we go to the Baptist church—and we're Christian, too.'"

"Amen, son, you answered her right." I wept with joy. Tears were coming down my cheeks.

When we got to the car, Ray and Amy asked what was the matter. "Children, your daddy's not crying because I'm sad. It's very obvious that I'm emotional. But your daddy's weeping because I'm so happy. And tonight when we read our Bible together before we go to sleep in the motel, daddy's going to tell y'all a story."

And that night I told them the story about my trip to Memphis, and their trip to Memphis, and what the difference was.

Jesus Christ makes a difference. This is one of the differences it made in my life. Praise God, it *was* a difference. Every child's got the right to get off of a train and their daddy meet them—and their daddy be rational and sound and show his love by the way he treats them.

It bothers me when I hear people say, "He's being treated like a stepchild." My stepfather loves the grandkids and they love him as much as blood kin. We've never at any time under any circumstances had a cross word, and we've been involved in some deals where I owed him a lot of money at times. He is a very conservative fellow, and if we were ever going to have any squabbles, it would have been over money. But we never did. And I don't owe him a dime today, praise the Lord.

But if I called him today and needed something, he'd send it to me. That's a good feeling.

He always had time for us children. Being the only boy, he might have had a little more time for me on occasion, but he always would go back and try to make up for it with the girls. He never lied to us. We were given the straight facts at all times.

He has set a great example for me. It wasn't so much how he *told* me to live as how he *lived* it. Very seldom would he tell me how to act. He let me decide for myself—and most of the time I'd just use how daddy would act in the situation and try to go at it like that.

I don't care how sorry anybody ever was, he'd say, "There's enough of that fellow left to salvage —let's go see what we can do." Daddy is just an ol' big-hearted country fellow. And he'd give anybody anything.

I had a professor in junior college who asked, "Ray, what's it like to be the son of a millionaire?" I told him, "I don't know. Whether my daddy had a hundred dollars in his pocket or one dollar, he has always been the same and lived the same. Success hasn't changed the real Jerry Clower."

One of the biggest lessons I've learned from my father is this: He says we don't have to agree, but we don't have to be disagreeable about it.

RAY CLOWER

4

How I Backed into
Show Business

WHEN I GOT out of Mississippi State with a degree in agriculture, I got a job just as I had planned to do: assistant county agent in charge of 4-H Club work. The first job I ever had was at Oxford, Mississippi—Lafayette County, the home of Ole Miss.

My hobby has been telling country stories—even while in service. Somebody would be talking about something and I'd tell them about how we used to do it when I was a kid growing up in southwest Mississippi. I started that in high school, except I didn't have many folks to tell stories to then because that's when they were happening. When I got off in the service, I started telling folks, and people would laugh at some of the things we did. I'd get transferred to another ship, and I'd remember those stories that folks laughed at and I'd entertain them a little bit sitting on the peacoat locker.

We moved to Oxford and had lived there a year when Pfister Associated Growers came through one day and gave me a sample of seed corn. I talked them out of enough to plant a patch for some needy kids in the county. This impressed them, and they came back not too long after that and hired me to be sales representative for Pfister in the state of Mississippi. We moved to Clarksdale. I still told country stories. I would go out to dealer meetings for this company, and they'd say, "Here's Jerry Clower—he used to play football at Mississippi State." I'd get up and tell the coonhunting story or something. I was in the hybrid seed corn business for two years at Clarksdale where my son Ray was born.

In January, 1954, I was in Jackson, Mississippi. They paged me at the old Heidelberg Hotel, and one of the old guys said, "How much did you pay them to call your name out in the lobby here?" I went to the phone. It was Owen Cooper, head of Mississippi Chemical Corporation. I had heard great things of Owen Cooper because he was an outstanding Baptist Christian and a very wonderful man. Twenty years later I had the opportunity to go to Philadelphia, Pennsylvania, and nominate him as president of the Southern Baptist Convention. And he won it, too. That's one of the things I did that I really felt the Lord wanted me to do.

"You've been recommended by the president of Mississippi State University," Mr. Cooper said. "I called him and asked for the name of a man who could make us a good field representative—a guy who can sell stock to get money to expand Mississippi Chemical and also sell fertilizer."

"I'm not interested. I got a good job selling seed corn." So I called my stepfather, Elliott Moore, and told him what I had done.

"Jerry, you made a mistake."

"What do you mean I made a mistake? Do you think I ought to take the job?"

"No, but *talk* about it. You may make a new friend in Owen Cooper whether you go to work for him or not; so don't ever make up your mind without the facts."

I called Mr. Cooper and went for an appointment. After he told me about the job and salary, I knew I had to take it. We moved from Clarksdale to Yazoo City, and I went to work as field representative for Mississippi Chemical on March 1, 1954. I worked southwest Mississippi, and before I was finished, I served some time in every field district of the company, and was later promoted to director of field services.

When I started working for Mississippi Chemical I'd go to a meeting and get up and tell those folks how we made homogenized, water-soluble, pelletized, chemically mixed fertilizers. And after making one of those talks I never did get invited back. So I started working in some of those country stories in my speeches wherever I'd go. Then I got invited back every time.

In 1970 in Point Cedar, Alabama, at the old Grand Hotel I was doing a performance for the Alabama Dairy Convention. Here I was doing public relations work as sales manager for Mississippi Chemical at the state dairy convention because they really use fertilizer. My talent motivated people to use our product.

After I finished entertaining, a guy ran up to me. "Why don't you make a record?"

"You're crazy. I'm a fertilizer peddler, and good at it."

"You ain't got nothing to lose, you're going to tell these blooming stories anyhow."

The next three or four times I went out to do a job-related speech, I asked some of the field representatives, who knew what a cassette tape recorder was, to tape it. One that I taped was at the state Farmers' Cooperative Convention in Corpus Christi, Texas. A guy taped it for me, and I mailed it to Roy Hatten in Jackson who was an after-dinner speaker. He said he'd take those tapes to a studio in Memphis and let the guy hear them. In the meantime, I was going to Lubbock, Texas, to sell some fertilizer, and I ran into Big Ed Wilkes who was farm director of KFYO radio. He came down to my room with a tape recorder. In talking to him, I told him the coon-hunting story.

"Man, you ought to make a record. We'll set the thing up."

I wrote Roy Hatten and told him to send the tapes back to me. He had enough time to do something with them, but nothing happened. When he returned the tapes, I sent them to Big Ed Wilkes out in Lubbock. He listened to them even though they weren't record quality.

"I think you ought to make an album."

They set up a catering service thing in Lubbock and invited a few friends. I got up and told the stories for about an hour. They pressed it into an album and put it on the Lemon label. That pleased me because I had heard the Beatles was Apple and I wanted to be Lemon.

Big Ed and his partner Bud Andrews printed up some envelopes and gave them to me. Wherever I'd go for a job-related talk—like the Farm Bureau of Pike County, Mississippi, or the Alabama Cattlemen's Association—I'd say, "By the way, some of these stories I told are on record. Here's an envelope. Put your return address and five dollars in this envelope and mail it off, and you get one of my albums." It wasn't long until we sold eight thousand of these albums at five dollars apiece.

Ed Wilkes mailed the "Yazoo City Talkin" album to farm directors he knew. John McDonald of WSM, Nashville, a friend of his, took the album and gave it to Grant Turner.

I carried the album around under my arm for two weeks, wondering what I was going to do with it. I had heard some of it, and I knew if I put it down that somebody would take it home with them. This had some stuff on it that everybody ought to hear.

GRANT TURNER

One Friday night after the Grand Ole Opry, Grant Turner played the coon hunt on WSM. Well, folks, that thing busted loose, and we got so many orders for the album that we couldn't fill them. They said, "What are we going to do?"

"I ain't going to do nothing. I've told you from the outset that I'm a very simple fellow. I live twenty-four hours at a time, and I ain't going to get hot and bothered about no album. If that don't suit y'all, I'm sorry, but that's the way I've been running my business ever since I was a sophomore at Mississippi State."

The next day, the boys in Lubbock got a feeler from a big record company in New York. Then MCA Records called. They flew to where we were, made a deal, and I signed with Music Corporation of America—MCA. Then "Yazoo City Mississippi Talkin'" retailed a million dollars' worth in the next ten months and got into the top twenty in *Billboard* and stayed there about thirty consecutive weeks. Then it busted loose. This is when I knew the Lord had let me back into show business.

After I got on MCA, so many people contacted me to do shows or put on promotions that I didn't know what in the world I was going to do. Man, I was having a rough time. Agencies were calling me from Nashville. About that time I was asked to do the *Nashville Banner* Sports Banquet.

> I was very much impressed with him at the banquet. He's a terrific speaker—I could hear him every day. He does an excellent job. I know he's a great humorist . . . very entertaining . . . and I understand he's a fine Christian man.
> COACH PAUL "BEAR" BRYANT

The next day Tandy Rice was reading the paper and called up Fred Russell, vice-president and sports director of the *Banner:* "This guy Jerry Clower—man, he's a hoss. Clower is a wower. He needs some management—it's very obvious he's got some talent." Then he called Ralph Emery, and Ralph said, "Look, I was there, and it beat everything I'd ever seen. He had nine hundred people in the palm of his hand."

Tandy called me, and I told him I could run my own business. "I'm a business executive. I supervise thirty-three men selling a hundred million dollars' worth of fertilizer annually, so don't be telling me that I need anybody to run my business."

The following Monday night, MCA got me on the David Frost show in New York City. David Frost said, "You're so refreshing and so different. Can you stay over tomorrow night?" I did the David Frost show on a Monday and Tuesday. The week those shows were broadcast on national TV, I was invited for a guest appearance on the Friday night Opry and both shows of the Saturday night Opry.

With the two David Frost shows, a front-page article in *MidSouth* magazine, and the Opry appearances, I got two hundred phone calls the following Monday. That was the week I decided I had to do something. My soul, Lord, what's happening to me? Lord, I'm still on your side . . . I ain't trying to run nothing . . . I'm just willing for you to use me.

I called Tandy Rice. "I've got to have some help— I see what you mean. I can't do this thing on my own, and I'm going to decide in the next two weeks what agency I'm going to sign with. I'm going to pray about it."

Two weeks later I called him. Some of my people and professional folks with other agencies were telling me whom I should go with, and Rice was a small agency, and you might oughta go with one of the big folks who have a tie-in with the movies. I found out later that's mostly talk more than anything else about how those folks can impress you about tying in with the movies. I heard some of those movie folks recently waiting to listen to a country superstar's record to find out who he was—and he's been with that agency for a long time.

"Look, I'm signing with you," I told Tandy. "I'm throwing in with you lock, stock, and barrel."

He came to Yazoo City the next day, brought a contract, and I signed it. The young men in Lubbock, they're fine folks. I love them. But at this point, I saw that I had outgrown Lubbock. I hadn't outgrown my friends. This was the first thing in show business I was feeling bad about. They couldn't understand why they couldn't continue exclusively to work with me on the records and Tandy work with me exclusively on the other part—but there's no way you can separate them. Show business is show business, and every day things would come up that I needed to answer, and the logistics of the thing . . . I couldn't get in touch with Lubbock.

I wanted Tandy Rice—a professional—to run the thing. I have utmost faith in him. Looking back on my career, the thing that has caused me to come this far so fast is, number one, to be on a prestigious record label, MCA, and, number two, to have fantastic management. Not only am I booked by Top Billing, but Tandy is my manager.

When we met for the first time in Yazoo City, it was sort of a magical mating. I was tremendously excited about him and his potential *then*. I am even more excited *today*. From that day, when he and I stacked hands and committed to each other . . . to the present time . . . my enthusiasm for him and what we were setting out to do has grown each day. It knows no bounds. I'm thankful for this enthusiasm I have for him. In the early days, it sustained me and was the most meaningful thing I had to fall back on. I truly and literally believe in him as much as it is possible for a person to believe in anything. And he has never let me down.

An interesting aspect of our relationship is how it has endured the test of time. He has *never* second-guessed me, or failed to do anything I've asked him to, or complained, or failed to say "thank you," or failed to say good things about me and our office staff and our efforts in his behalf. It's a good feeling to share such a positive working relationship with someone. To know that no matter where he is, or what he's doing, he is telling somebody something great about me and my fellow workers back in Nashville. He's devoted to us. We are devoted to him.

The potential of his career hasn't even been halfway fulfilled. I have three goals for him. One, preserve his physical and mental well-being through sensible and controlled career development. Two, make him financially secure for life —he has the potential for easily becoming a millionaire. And, three, develop him into a major humorist with *national* renown in much the same respect as Andy Griffith and Flip Wilson.

All of these goals can be realized. I can see light at the end of the tunnel.

TANDY RICE
President, Top Billing Agency
and Personal Manager of Jerry Clower

I'm a spendthrift, I give money, I'm a soft touch, and I tithe my income—I've done that all my life. But over and above my tithe—my offering—sometimes I give too much. I've given money I don't even have. I've borrowed money to give to poor folks. I've borrowed money to pay off my pledge at the church. A lot of folks don't understand why I do that. But if I pledged at the Buick place and they wanted the money, I'd have to come up with it; so if I pledge to God, I'd better come up with it, too. The most important business I'm engaged in ought to be the Lord's business. If it ain't, I need to get off and classify myself and see whose side I'm on.

Everything is beautiful. I'm on the MCA label, and I signed with Tandy Rice. In the last year, I've done over two hundred performances. For the last two years,

I've been selected as the Country Comic of the Year. I'm a competitor. I was the number one fertilizer salesman in the world; so if I'm going to get into anything, I'm going to do the best I can. When Bill Anderson writes about the top country comic in the nation, he says Jerry Clower. So do *Record World, Billboard,* and *Cash Box.*

Every time I see him, he surprises me because he's maturing so fast as an entertainer. He hasn't really scratched the surface yet—his potential keeps building. As time goes on, he's smoothing out. He doesn't use dirty jokes, and his humor seems to be endless. It's good that he can accomplish that with all the so-called dirty type of comedy that has taken over. When comedians start dealing in filth, it just gets filthier and filthier. You don't find any of that at all in Jerry's material. Yet he's a nice guy to be around. You don't have to feel cramped. You can speak what you feel.

Jerry is liked by a lot of the people who frequent the bars and clubs, and he's also liked by people in other walks of life. He handles it very well being able to bridge both audiences.

I'm very proud of what's happened, and I'm very proud to know him. He has been a very good addition to our family.

OWEN BRADLEY
Vice-President, MCA Records
and member of the Country Music
Hall of Fame

When all this started happening to me, Owen Cooper and Charles J. Jackson—my immediate boss at Mississippi Chemical—told me one day, "What's happening to you could be unbelievable, or it could blow over and not amount to anything. But we're willing to share you for a while until you see which way the thing's going."

This is working for Christian management and working for a company with a heart. That's part of me being successful. If they would have said, "Look, make up your mind which way you're going—you're either going to be show business or running the outside domestic sales of this company—make up your mind," I might not have taken the chance of pursuing show business. They told me, "If this show business thing grows to where you don't think you can do your job, you recommend what you think we need to do."

One day I walked in the office and said, "This thing has gotten to where I can't do an adequate job for Mississippi Chemical and be in show business too. I would like to name my replacement, Mr. R. Douglas Hall from Atmore, Alabama. I suggest you bring him in and make him director of field services. I'll move out of the office and move over yonder into another office, and you can call me anything you want to call me and cut my salary commensurate with the duties I'm giving up."

"We'll do that, and we'll make you sales promotion director. You can do enough shows annually at big dealer meetings and where our field men suggest you come."

That's what I do. I'm still sales promotion director, but technically I don't have anything to do with the company other than occasionally making a public appearance for them. It's a real good deal for me, and it works out great for Mississippi Chemical, too. More than anything else at my office, I sign autographed pictures for fans—and pick up my airline ticket. Mrs. Judy Moore who was my secretary when I ran the field staff was allowed to continue helping me. She keeps my records for expenses and taxes and scheduling. I leave there and do ten shows in ten nights before I come back. I catch a different airplane each time— and you can see how thick my ticket is and how much problem she has on motels and hotels, and every town you go to you have a press conference and you're interviewed at the radio station and TV station, and she keeps up with all that. She does a great job. I've been careful not to put too much on her because Barbara Farnsworth—one of the finest secretaries in the world—represents me at Top Billing.

One day I'm sitting in the office at Yazoo City and the phone rings. "Mr. Clower, I'm Marshall Rowland. I own a radio station in Jacksonville, Florida. I was driving to work this morning and heard the chain-saw story. This is big pulpwood country, and that's the funniest thing I've ever heard in my life. We're having a Charley Pride Show down here in about two weeks. If you fly down here, I'll pay your expenses and pay you something. We're playing your album, and this will help you sell some records, I'd like to say we got the man that made the chain-saw record."

So I went down there and got out to the big coliseum and found out that Charley Pride's manager didn't want me on the show. This was another side of show business that I didn't know anything about. I often wondered why the man didn't want me on the show when it wasn't my fault.

Marshall Rowland brought me on about ten minutes to eight while all the popcorn folks were still selling popcorn and the hawkers were selling programs and people were still hunting their seats. I came out and went for ten minutes, and I told the chain-saw and the coon-hunt. Later, backstage, Jack Johnson—Charley Pride's manager—got to talking to me and found out that I was invited by Marshall Rowland who was the local guy running the show. The next night we were going to do the same show in Tampa. Apparently Mr. Johnson started liking me or understood the situation a little better because they brought me on at eight o'clock. I started the show, followed by the Glaser Brothers, Bill Anderson, and Charley Pride.

I had bought me a coat to wear for the show—I didn't know about show clothes. Backstage, there was Bill Anderson. I had seen him on television and, being a country music fan, I knew about him and loved his work. "Bill Anderson, I'm Jerry Clower. I'm the guy that tells the stories."

"Good to see you."

I had never heard of him. This guy was wearing a sport coat exactly like the one I had bought two days earlier. I immediately disliked him. I was mad at him. Instantly. I said, "How dare him to have a coat exactly like mine." The guys in the band were teasing me because they thought he was a fan or something. They said, "You'll look out there in the audience tonight and see about ten of those coats just like that."

Jerry's reaction was so fantastic it knocked me out. He said, "You mean I got the good taste to buy a coat exactly like the great Bill Anderson?"

How can you be mad at somebody like that?

                                        BILL ANDERSON

The next morning I went to have breakfast in the motel. Now I don't like to do anything by myself. I don't like to eat, travel, nothing by myself. If I can be with folks, I want to be with them. That's why I don't hunt or fish by myself—I love to talk with folks. I saw a guy sitting in the restaurant and walked over to him. "Sir, I'm perfectly harmless. Can I sit here and eat breakfast with you?"

It was Jimmy Gately. From that day to this one we started being buddies. What united us was that he had kids the age of mine. We shared the way we counseled and disciplined our children.

Bill Anderson came by and asked how I was going to travel to the next show. "Well, I'm going to catch the airplane or rent a car."

"Would you like to ride over there with me on my bus?"

"Thank you very much." After I got on that bus and sat down, Bill asked me to tell some stories. I started telling them and he ended up on the floor, hollering and whooping.

He started telling stories before we got out of the city limits. I remember twice my bus driver had to actually pull the bus over on the side of the road and stop, he was laughing so hard.

BILL ANDERSON

Since then I've met Bill's daddy, Mr. Jim Anderson —a wonderful Methodist layman at Decatur, Georgia. Out of my love for him, I've spoken in his church twice as a Christian entertainer. The Bill Anderson family I would classify as close friends—and you don't have many close friends in this world.

Bill asked me to be on his TV show. He's the first artist to give me a big boost in show business.

About a week after signing with MCA, I was listening to Ralph Emery on WSM, and Bill was sitting in. I called him. "Bill, would you believe I have just signed with MCA?"

"I'm so glad. They don't have a humorist on their label. I'm sure we'll be working closer together now because I'll be seeing you around Bradley's Barn and MCA Records in Nashville."

One of the highlights of my show business career was being asked to join the world famous Grand Ole Opry. To me that was the biggest honor I've had in show business because when I was asked to join the Opry I hadn't been in show business two years, but I had two hit albums and they were going strong. I had done some guest appearances on the Opry, and there wasn't an exclusive stand-up comic on it.

The sixty-fourth member of the Grand Ole Opry. And Governor Waller coming up to represent the State of Mississippi, Tandy Rice having a big feed, and Roy Blount Jr. of *Sports Illustrated* came down to participate. Woooo!

After WSM started playing my album, I was listening to them one night, and Ralph Emery was talking about Wendy Bagwell who had recently been up there to visit: "That Jerry Clower, I've never met him, but if I could get Jerry Clower and Wendy Bagwell on the same show, we'd have a good time. John Riggs is here with me—and you call our number for a request." Well, I kept calling. Little Katy had just been born and she was sleeping in our bedroom, and I was laying over by her on a cot, listening to that radio. The number was busy, so I kept dialing. Directly I got through.

"This is Jerry Clower. I'm the man that made the coon-hunt record and I want to talk to Ralph Emery."

"Hold on just a minute," John Riggs answered.

"Hello!" Ralph Emery said.

"God bless your WSM soul!"

"Pardon?"

"This is Jerry Clower. Whooooo . . . shoot this thang!"

"That's a great record. When do you want to come see me?"

"When can I come?"

"Any time you want to."

I checked my fertilizer-selling schedule and got up there one night and stayed with him all night long. That was my first test of really sitting in with a disk jockey.

"Jerry, you ought to be invited to do a guest appearance on the Grand Ole Opry."

"Man, I couldn't stand it. When I was a little boy, I used to pray that we'd clear enough money at the end of the crop year to where we could go see the world famous Grand Ole Opry. I never have been. And you mean to tell me if I could do a guest appearance on the Opry, and the first time I ever saw the Opry I would have performed on it . . . Woooo! man, I can't stand it!"

"It'd be real simple you getting on there."

"It would?"

"Yeah. Owen Bradley at MCA—he's kind of a

heavy in the music business. All Owen's got to do is pick up the phone and call Bud Wendell."

Ralph must have been right. The record company told me I was scheduled to perform as a guest on the Opry. That was an unbelievable night. All my life— being in sales—I'm real sensitive about being on time. I got there about an hour early. I asked how long I had on stage, and Bud Wendell told me how many minutes, and added, "If you go thirty seconds or a minute over that—it's fine. But if you go longer than that, we'll bring the hook out and get you."

On the Grand Ole Opry, I got my first taste of knowing what an audience wanted. Tex Ritter—God bless him—brought me out: "Here's a young man who has made the sport of coon hunting famous."

When he said that—before he even mentioned my name—people in the audience hollered, "Knock him out, John," and I heard another fellow holler, "Wooo, shoot this thang." I had been standing backstage thinking up a story that had never been told on record. I *knew* you couldn't tell an audience what you told on record—they had already heard it. But then it dawned on me. Here was a crowd of people waiting to hear what was the most popular thing being played on the radio. If Loretta Lynn went to do a show and didn't do her record which was the most popular right then, they'd turn the stage over.

So let's face it. The fans make it easy for you. It's simple for me to tell the coon hunt—I've told it nine jillion times. It's gotten to where now I can't do a show anywhere where they don't demand that I tell the coon hunt. If they heard it driving down to the auditorium, they want to hear Jerry Clower tell the coon hunt again. A guy asked me if I thought I could make it forever just on the coon hunt story. I don't have to. I have a lot of other good stories. But I could if I had to because I know a fellow who has made it pretty well on the "Wabash Cannonball."

So while I was walking out and Tex Ritter was

introducing me, I thought: these people want to hear the coon hunt. I believe I'll tell it.

I told it. And I encored. They hollered and hooted and screamed. When I came back, one of them in the audience yelled, "Marr-cellll!" So I cut out on the chain-saw story.

Then I was invited several other times to be a guest on the Opry. That's where I met Jeanne Pruett—she was making a few guest appearances on the Opry. I was thrilled to death to have an opportunity to do a guest appearance the night Jeanne was inducted into the Opry. She's a very lovely person—a fine mother, a wonderful entertainer, and a great songwriter. It was the greatest event in her show business career, and I was so proud for her. Then I was the next one to be asked to join the Opry, but at that time I didn't even know it. Jeanne was just as happy that I was inducted as I was when she joined.

There's a fraternal love among recording artists. When Bill Williams of *Billboard* wrote me a letter and said I was the first country artist in the history of show business to put a talking record in the top ten of the nation, Jeanne heard about it and cried with joy. She came to my Amy's wedding—and "Satin Sheets" was number one in the nation that day. Jeanne came walking up with a pair of king-sized satin bedsheets. Three nurses slipped off from the Yazoo City Hospital just to come over to my house and see Jeanne Pruett. On Christmas Eve night, I'm sitting at the table with my family when the phone rings. I pick it up and this voice sings, "We wish you a Merry Christmas . . ." It was Jeanne calling my family to sing Merry Christmas to us.

I'm a country performer. But this doesn't shame me. Because country folks have never had it so good.

I did the theater-in-the-round on tour in Washington, D.C., Cleveland, Ohio, and Boston, Massachusetts. It took a lot of guts to put me in Boston. In Cleveland, you would have thought my mama wrote the reviews. The reviewer wrote about how I could actually tell funny stories about myself and didn't have to put anybody down, cut anybody, or be ugly to anyone to get a laugh.

Clower, a big 270-pound ex-football player, is a refreshing change from that sickly string of comedians who desperately crave laughs apparently for neurotic reasons. Instead, Clower is a humorist who tells true stories about himself that are honestly funny.

You feel that, inside, Clower is a rock, a man of strong character, a religious man with convictions. He spins yarns about going raccoon hunting and treeing a lynx, about seeing his first college football game—a game in which he also played—and about trying to be chivalrous to Gloria Steinem. (She grew furious that he offered his chair. She sat on the floor instead.)

"We growed up a lot different," he told his city folk audience. "But I ain't going to make fun of how you come up."

The audience wasn't about to make fun of him —or of country music, either. The audience was too busy enjoying it all.

DICK WOOTEN
Cleveland Press

During theater-in-the-round in Washington, Mr. Lee Goober—who is the he-coon of the whole thing —had fresh flowers and fruit delivered to my room every night. First Class. The sign said, "Merle Haggard Show with Special Guest Star, Jerry Clower."

I figured I'd go twenty minutes and bring on the Strangers and they'd go twenty and then have intermission, and then Merle Haggard. They told me to go forty-five minutes. That's a long time for a stand-up comic in a Northern town. I hit that stage like a flying jenny—going round and round. Theater-in-the-round. There were a lot of women in the audience so I bragged on women, treed the raccoon, and forty-five minutes later I got a standing ovation. I ran off the stage, and Mr. Lee Goober came back to my dressing room saying, "Look, I don't believe this. I don't believe this at all."

"Sir?"

"I'm not believing this. We just had some other nationally known comedians, and they'd go twenty minutes. Man, you went forty-five minutes and you didn't even say a four-letter word."

"That's what makes these folks love me. I got enough talent to entertain folks without being vulgar. Ain't that great?"

"It is . . . but I didn't think there was anybody who could do it."

Well, here's a new album, "Country Ham," by Jerry Clower. Isn't it wonderful that I don't have to take this in a back room and listen to it. I can just put it on—anything by Jerry Clower you know you can play on the air. Let's just play this cut, "The She-Coon of Women's Lib." This is the first time I've ever heard it.

disk jockey MONTY DUPUY
on the air at WFBC, Greenville, South Carolina

In between shows at Columbia, South Carolina, a guard came backstage. "Mr. Clower, there's a boy out here wants to see you, but we can't let him backstage. He's crying. His daddy brought him a hundred miles to see you."

"Let me go out there." He was outside sitting up on a fire escape with his head in his little hands. He was about five. "Hey, son, you come to see me?"

He stood up, and he was even with my face because he was standing on the fire escape. He grabbed me around the neck, hugged me, and cried, "Oh, Jerry, Jerry, you're the only one I come to saw."

His daddy explained, "We live a hundred miles from here, but my son heard on the radio that you were going to be here, and he begged me to bring him."

Now wouldn't it be a sin before God if I were the type of entertainer who told stories that were such that little Mike Sanders couldn't love me?

There must have been thirty kids at Panama City, Florida, for my show. I stayed and signed autographs for them. I get mail from speech teachers all over the country who say, "Is it all right for one of our kids to tell your stories?" They must know something about ASCAP. Most of them just go on and tell the stories—which is beautiful. They don't need my permission. I don't care. The more my stories are told, the more records it sells. But it shows the teachers are teaching them something about respect for other people's stuff when they write me a letter asking, "Can this boy say the coon hunt? . . . If you give him permission, he's going to tell it, and I'm going to give him a grade on it." I write him right back: "Son, tell it. I hope you make a hundred."

I get letters from kids everywhere. One of the big ambitions I've got is to someday do a children's album. Sit down with a bunch of kids and talk to them and tell stories. My little kid every night asks, "Daddy, tell me the coon hunt." She's heard it a jillion times. And I make up a bunch of stories just for her that I should have put on record long ago.

> I like my daddy a lot. He's a good father. He
> takes me riding around sometimes when he's at
> his house. He tells me about Little Red, and he
> tells me lots of coon hunt stories.
>
> KATY CLOWER

In Magnolia, Arkansas, they told me, "One of your biggest fans called and said he wants to see you." Soon they came rolling a wheelchair, and there was a spastic boy. They put a walker down and he grabbed it. His shoulders and arms were like Tarzan's from the exercise of pulling himself up. He said, "Mr. Clower, I love you. I got me a ticket to the show tonight and it's a sell-out, and ten people have tried to buy my ticket from me. But I wouldn't get rid of it for anything."

I grabbed him, picked him up, and hugged him. Everybody standing around was crying. I held to him and said, "You love me and I love you. If listening to my records gives you any kind of happiness, it's worth it all."

I got his name and address and wrote on the bottom of a note to Tandy Rice: "Rice-marize." If I tell him to Rice-marize anybody, the person gets a Knock'em Out John Award, T-shirts, pictures, and other gifts. One of the joys of show business is that this young man loves me, and instead of worrying about his trembling feet and shaking body, he spends some of his time listening to my albums. If my stories can give him some enjoyment and take his mind off his problem and onto the things I've talked about, then that's beautiful. I love it.

Working for a very fine company for so long, I knew a little something about how businesses ought to be run. I'd fly to a town for a package show, arrive at the auditorium, and the buyer and promoter of the show would say, "When do you want to go on and how much time do you want?"

"Sir, I have hired out to you. You tell me how much time you want me to take and you tell me what portion in the show you want me to go on, and I'll do the best job for you I possibly can."

"Whew! No wonder you're booked up months ahead and it's so hard to book you."

I didn't know what he meant until later when I heard him ask another artist the same questions and the artist wanted to go on at a certain time and he just took over and tried to change the whole show. I was flabbergasted that the bossman would let an artist run his show.

People say it's ego; I don't know what it is. I like to work for folks who are firm and know what they

want and tell you what to do. A perfect example of
this is the Minnesota State Fair. You get there and
they hand you a mimeographed sheet that tells you
when you go on and how long you take—and it's not
discussable or debatable. That's the way it is—and
that's why this man, John Libby, runs one of the best
fairs in all the world. You don't run him. He runs
you. He ought to run it—he's paying you.

The only difference I see in Mr. Clower from when
he was selling fertilizer to now is that he's got a
lot more pictures hanging on his wall.

K. K. HILL
son of Chief Carey Hill and Marguerite Hill

5

Questions and Answers

EVERYWHERE I GO, I'm asked a lot of questions; so I'll take this opportunity to answer a few of them here.

The most prevalent question I'm asked is, "Did you really play football like your album says?"

Yes. I did not play in high school because I finished school with just seven other folks. There were eight of us in the senior class. Although I told them I was "the man what runs with the football," it didn't take the college coaches very long to find out I wasn't a running back. It doesn't shame me that I played tackle because how would you like to see them run the off-tackle play without a tackle? Ha ha ha! They would have those ambulances lined up hauling them to the hospital—one right behind another.

The football playing has really been good to me because I have capitalized on it by telling some stories on record and stage about my football-playing days. Like the time Mississippi State played Kentucky, and I ran to the sidelines and screamed in a loud voice, "Time out!"

58

"Boy, what in the world's the matter?"

"That Kentucky team ain't playing fair. That Babe Parilli, their quarterback, has got three footballs—and that ain't fair. He's giving one of them to the half-back, one to the fullback, and he's chunking one. And if y'all are going to let Kentucky play with three footballs, let us play with three."

They had kind of a smart-aleck referee there, and he said, "You ain't doing too well with the one you got."

The second most prevalent question I'm asked wherever I go is, "What do you think about the young people of today?"

Even David Frost asked me this question when I was on his show. "Do you think the young people of today are better or worse than they were when you were growing up?"

"Mr. Frost, I think they're better now."

"Oh? What makes you say that?"

"Because 2 percent of the kids today are sorry, but 98 percent of them are good. It bothers me a little that the TV folks talk about the 2 percent that are bad a lot more than they talk about the 98 percent that are good."

"Are you sure?"

"Well, I believe I'm reasonably sure because I've got a teen-age son of my own and I guarantee you, my son Ray is a lot better boy now than I was when I was growing up. In fact, when I was the same age that my son is now, if I would have had one of them new LeSabre Buicks, not only would I have stole them watermelons, but I would have gotten away with them!"

When I spoke to the humanities class of a great teacher and woman—Mrs. Harriet DeCell—I was spellbound by the ability of the kids to ask questions. Some of the bright black kids asked penetrating questions. That's why I can hardly wait to turn this country over to some of the young people. I'd take the top ten

students at Vanderbilt University today and replace
the bottom ten of the president's cabinet in the morning
if I had the opportunity to do it. In fact, I might take
five students to replace ten of them.

The number three most asked question is: "Did
Marcel Ledbetter *really* tear up that beer joint? Is he
real? And did McCulloch Chain Saw pay you to say
McCulloch on that record?"

The story I tell about Marcel is that he was driving
his pulpwood truck back out to the East Fork Community after a hard day's work, and that hot evening
sun was staring him right in the face. Now Amite
County is dry. The people have never voted in any
kind of alcoholic beverage. If you want to get a cool
one, you have to ride over on the county line where
they've got a joint. Marcel had good Christian teach-
ings, and he knew better than to buy any of them cool
beers. But he knew also that they had those big Nehi
belly-washers—and they were cold. He wanted one of
them so bad. He eased his pulpwood truck over off
the paved highway. Now all he had on between him
and the Lord was just a pair of overalls. That's all.
He was barefooted. He did have the bottom button on
the sides buttoned; the top buttons were flapping. He
eased up to this tavern, looked through the screen door,
and said, "Hey."

The man behind the counter said, "What you want?"

"Would you hand me a cold soda water?"

"You better get away from that door—go get you
a shirt on, get you on some clothes. We don't want
the likes of you in here."

"I ain't coming in. All I want you to do is hand me
a cold soda water through the door, and I'll pay you
for it and pay you for the old bottle, and I'll drink it
while I'm driving home."

Four fellows were sitting around a table playing
cards. One of them said, "Didn't you hear him tell you
to get away from that door, you redneck?"

Poor old Marcel, walking on that gravel out there,

went back to his truck and reached in the tool box and brought out one of those lightweight McCulloch chain saws. He reached down and took ahold of that starting rope and . . . WAAAAAAA! He walked up to the door of that beer joint and just stuck the snout of that thing through the screen door. WAAAOOOOOM! WAAWAAMMM! He reamed him out a hole in that screen door, and eased it over to the side and it hung in that screen door. WOWOWAAPOWACH! He held it up over his head and revved it up to where all those screen wires and hinges and things came loose from it. WAWAACH! Then he stepped inside, raced the motor three or four times, and slung that thing at a table, and just took off two legs—and the table said WOP!

They gave Marcel the beer joint!

Now McCulloch does not advocate, and Jerry Clower does not advocate, that you use a chain saw like Marcel did. It really happened a couple of times in southwest Mississippi where I grew up. McCulloch did not pay me to say McCulloch on that record because I didn't know I was going to say it. When I told the story live before an audience and it was being taped for a record, it just slipped out. It's a very fine compliment on the McCulloch Corporation that when I thought of a saw, I thought of theirs. I'm not going to lie to you. I want everybody to know who's reading this book that I some kind of love them. I'm glad now that I said McCulloch on that record because old man McCulloch flew me to Hollywood and Tandy Rice worked out a deal with them where I'm on retainer for them. In fact, McCulloch has been good enough to me that I got to telling my wife that we ought to figure out what kind of dog food we fed those coon dogs. Wooo! If anybody was wondering, it was High Protein Purina Dog Meal —that's what kind it was.

Yes, Marcel is real. I purposely don't identify a particular person and say he's Marcel because it could be one or two or three people. I let people guess. Down the road I'm going to let Marcel do a lot of other things

—like his snuff gives him indigestion, and what we did at a Tarzan picture one time.

When me and Marcel were growing up, we just loved them Tarzan picture shows. The mail rider would tell us whenever there was a Tarzan picture show on. So me and Marcel hitchhiked to town, got a pound of butter to sell to get into the show, and sold it to the guy that pops the popcorn out in front of the theater. When the movie started, the lights went off and the lion went on ARRRRCHHH!—Metro Goldwyn Mayer ARRRCCHHH! Marcel jumped up and shouted, "Roar! Roar! You scoundrel, you. Tarzan will be out there in a minute and tear you up!"

Two weeks later we were back at the theater, and the guy wouldn't give us but twenty-five cents for a pound of butter—we wanted thirty cents. This guy said, "Marcel, did you bring more cheap butter to town? I sure would be interested. That was fine on our hot biscuits." Marcel told him, "I ain't going to have no more butter that cheap. In fact, you wouldn't have got this butter that cheap if the cat hadn't of fell in the churn."

One of these days I may do an album—"Me and Marcel." It would be things I've done with a lot of people, but I'd let Marcel do them all.

Speaking of Marcel and young people, we were taught better manners than young people are taught now, especially at the table. Back when I was growing up, food was scarcer, and we didn't have an abundant supply of certain items. When you bowed your head and asked the Lord to bless the food, you didn't mess over it. You ate what was on the table and you shut up. You didn't run out to McDonald's if you didn't like what they had. We were taught as kids that you didn't clean out any platter or dish. You didn't take the last helping of butterbeans out of the bowl, you didn't take the last fried sweet potato off the platter, you didn't take the last biscuit, or the last piece of chicken.

I worked up a routine concerning this truth. I tell the story of how I went over to Marcel's house about dark one evening to see if Uncle Virsi Ledbetter would let Marcel go coon hunting with me. When I walked in, there was the Ledbetter family all sitting around the supper table. They were very quiet and all of them were staring at the last piece of chicken on the platter. There they sat—Ardel, Bernel, Raynel, W. L., Lanel, Odel, and Marcel—just staring at the last piece of chicken on the platter. About that time the wind blowed the lamp out, and the room got black dark. "Haaachhhh!" Uncle Virsi squawled. And when Aunt Pet Ledbetter got the lamp relit, there were five forks sticking in the back of Uncle Virsi's hand.

The next question I'm asked is: "As an entertainer from Yazoo City, Mississippi, do people mistreat you when you do shows in the North?" The answer is no. Emphatically no.

Before I performed in Boston, one of my friends called to warn me that I should change my license tags if I planned to drive North. There's nothing to that. Hallelujah, there ain't no more North, South, East, and West in show business either. I hope and pray that we get this sectionalism done away with as far as America is concerned. I don't want folks to sell their birthright or lose their heritage, but I want America to be one great big country, and everybody as Americans, and everybody's loving one another and getting it on.

MCA selected me as one of the artists to perform on their West Coast music festival for record distributors from all over the world. Performing on the same show that night were Sonny and Cher. On the way out there, I decided they wouldn't like me—and I knew none of the Hollywood folks would like me. But I got to thinking: Jerry, your Rt. 4, southwest Mississippi carnal nature is coming down on you. You have overcome those days when you made up your mind that you didn't like people just because they dressed different than you did. You have overcome those days that you didn't like people just because their skin's a different color than yours. You have overcome those days that you used to decide you didn't like people because they had a funny name according to you. I said, "Lord, please forgive me. Here I am judging some of those Hollywood folks and stars before I investigate them as individuals and see if we can get along."

Well, I've never been treated so nice in all my life. Sonny and Cher, Ricky Nelson, all of the fine record executives out there, and especially Roger Williams, were so nice. I'll never be the same again.

People ask me about this cross I wear that also has the Star of David on it. I do a lot of shows with people who wear the Star of David and a lot with people who wear the cross. I believe what the Bible says about both of them. So I just had me one made.

I was doing the "Mike Douglas Show," and a lady from New York came up to me after the show, put on her glasses, got up real close, and asked, "I understand the cross, and I understand the Star of David, but why the carat diamond?"

"Well, lady, that represents the self-centeredness and hillbilly in me. And I'm trying to overcome it. Pray for me."

The idea came from Country Crossroads. I got a poster from them that had the Star of David with a cross behind it. Albriton's Jewelers in Jackson, Mississippi, made it for me after I showed them the poster. It's got a lot of people talking. I had a couple more made for Tandy Rice and Barbara Farnsworth—and it tickled them to death.

6

Race, Creed, and Christians

> Jerry ought not to be associating with those damn niggers.
>
> YAZOO CITY RESIDENT

I WAS RAISED in this community—and grew up a bigot and racist. When I was a little boy, a citizen told me he did not think a Negro had a soul, and then he told me a Republican was worse than that.

In boot camp at the Williamsburg, Virginia, navy base, I was sitting on a barracks bunk talking to a guy named Rutkowski. Two guys named Schmidt von Kallen and Gersky walked up. "Where's Clower?"

"Right heah."

"Come on over here with us. Gersky's mama just sent him some fine German food. We know you'll love it."

"What?"

"Come on over. You *are* Clower?"

"Yeah, I'm Clower."

"Well, come on over. You are German, aren't you?"

This embarrassed me. I didn't know what I was. "Man, where I come from you're either black or white. Period. There ain't no other kind of folks. And if I am German, I'm a molasses-and-biscuit German. I don't know nothing about them cookies and that Wiener schnitzel. And this sauerkraut—it stinks. I know I ain't going to eat none of that. Whoever heard of eating that? It smells like sour cabbage to me."

The barracks door opened and one of these boys from New Jersey said, "Look at those damn kikes."

"What?"

"Those Jews."

"Where?"

"Coming through the door of the barracks—can't you see them?"

"How can you tell?"

"My God, ha-ha-ha! Hey, come here, the rebel here from Mississippi doesn't know what a Jew is."

And that was the first time I ever realized you were supposed to be bigoted and hate folks other than black people. I was taught that in the North. I couldn't understand how they would have the audacity to say anything racist about a white man. And they'd tell me that I was no better than a black man—and it would make me furious. Then they would tell me they were better than a Jew, and I was ready to fight them.

Don't you see how stupid we were? Praise God, I have evaluated all of this, and, over the years, I have changed. Here's why.

The number one reason, to be perfectly honest, is that I worked for a very godly man, Owen Cooper. He literally was a Christian. He believed in religious freedom. He gave me the right to believe like I want to, and he would love me, and pray for me, regardless of how I believed.

Some people would have changed a little quicker if they thought they needed to make a change concerning their beliefs about race. But some folks work for bigots, for racists. To express themselves like they wanted, they might have gotten fired. I didn't have that hanging over my head.

Even back when I was a little boy, I would bring up to adults things that happened to black people. They said it was best not to discuss it. But it bothered me, and I was concerned about it all my life.

Some years ago, about the time we were having the civil rights marches and the restaurant sit-ins, I was in a store one day and saw a little black girl in her mother's arms crying, "I want a drink of water." The mother walked to the water fountain and leaned her baby over. A big guy walked up and said, "That nigger don't drink out of that fountain—move on!"

That's another reason I changed. All of my changing would always go back to my Christian faith. I would try to explain how I felt about it to the Lord. And I had a lot of friends and neighbors I could discuss it with.

Back when I first started selling fertilizer and was a full-blood bigot, some of my customers enjoyed seeing me coming because I'd tell stories about black people. Aw, they were funny, I thought back then. As I tried to explain how I felt about it while praying to God, I got more and more under conviction that I was doing wrong. As I prayed about it, I gradually changed. But the thing that really did it was when Mississippi Chemical hired a black field representative. I volunteered to supervise him, and it wasn't long until I found out that this man had a lot more sense than I did. We got to talking about the Lord to one another, and I found out that this man's wife had been in a mental institution for over twenty-five years—and this fine black man had been faithful to his wife for those twenty-five years. I don't know whether I could be faithful for twenty-five years to a lady after the doctor told me she wasn't ever going to get out of the mental institution. It would be tempting for Ol' Jerry.

So I started receiving people as individuals. As an individual, we might have nothing in common and I might want to have nothing to do with him, but at least I gave each individual an opportunity to be my friend.

After my brother Sonny retired as a commander from the navy, I asked what he would do different if he had to do it all over again while serving a long term in the navy. "Jerry, when I first got in the navy, I popped off about I was from Mississippi, and it ain't right for me to have to stay down here with these two black guys on this submarine. We hadn't no more than gotten out of port good when we took a hit, and both of those boys got killed. While they were burying them at sea, I got to thinking: There's a lot of white people on this submarine that I have found out we can't be friends because we don't believe anything alike. We'll just be acquaintances, but we won't grow to be buddies. But there wasn't a single individual on there that was white that I didn't go to the trouble of having a discussion or visit with him to see if he wanted to be my friend or if I wanted to be his friend. But I automatically culled the two black people just because they were black. When they replaced these two fellas, I made up my mind that I'm going to give every individual the right to be my friend, and not cull him just because he's black."

I thought a lot about what my brother said. There were times in my life when I automatically culled an individual because he wasn't white. As a Christian, I don't think I can do this and say that I'm a Christian. It just doesn't work that way.

A friend of mine has a plantation in the Mississippi Delta, and he decided to build some decent houses for his black tenants. He even worked up a system whereby they would be graded and given points as to which family kept their house looking the best. Naturally, he couldn't build a brick veneer home for every hand on his place at one time. But he built several, and each year he built a few more. There was a waiting list, and the ones who did the best job keeping the children in school, and personal hygiene, and living like citizens and human beings ought to live, got priority on moving into the good house. But when the man started the housing program, there were some people who actually burned crosses in his yard. They did not want these blacks living in adequate housing.

Some folks would say, Why do you want to even bring that up? Because it didn't happen too many years ago—and it's wrong.

One of the fashionable things to do today is for an individual to knock his past. I don't intend to do that. I think my folks did an excellent job under the circumstances with what they had to do it with. I grew up in a community that was instilled in a tradition for some two hundred years. We're making tremendous progress, and I'm thrilled about it. I was taught some things as a kid that I found out later weren't right. Not only about race, but about other things.

As a kid I used to help my grandfather drive up a cow that he had diagnosed as having the disease of Hollow Tail or Hollow Horn. I have literally helped split the cow's tail and treated it with salt, or cut her horns off because Big Daddy said they were hollow and she had the Hollow Horn. I thought this was a wonderful medical remedy until I attended Mississippi State University and had to take some courses in animal science before I could get a degree in agriculture. I was just flabbergasted to hear the professor in animal husbandry say there was no such thing as these diseases—that it was just a tradition and people should not have done this to these cows.

I challenged the professor. "Prof, you looka heah. I done helped my grandpa drive up these cows and I done slit their tail, and they always got better and looked better after we treated her by slitting her tail and cutting off her horns."

"While you were treating her for the Hollow Horn, did you keep the cow in a pen and feed her?"

"Yessir."

"Well, she had Hollow Belly. That was her problem. You kept the cow and fed her. She had Hollow Belly, not Hollow Tail."

Now we had been sincere. We thought we were

helping that cow, but we were sincerely wrong. This was a tradition taught by the older people and believed by some of the younger ones.

My grandpa also thought that coal oil would cure cancer. We used it as a cough syrup. We'd put two drops on a spoonful of sugar. We killed hogs and planted crops by the moon. A lot of these old ways I don't knock. In fact, I still believe in a lot of them because when I got to Mississippi State in the school of agronomy and studied those planting charts, I discovered my grandpa never did miss it a day as to when was the best time to plant crops.

In Yazoo City, Mississippi, the courts told us during Christmas holidays that we had to have one high school instead of separate schools for white and blacks. The court said: When you go back, you got one high school.

This tried everybody. This was something! If you can't lean on your Christian faith at a time like that, you can't lean at all.

So I sat down with my children and my wife, and as a Christian family we discussed what we were going to do. People were organizing private schools and getting them set up in some of the local churches. I thought this was great until I found out that nobody who was black could attend one of these schools. I told my son and daughter, "Look, here is a young man who lives in Yazoo City, he made one of the highest grades on the ACT test ever made in high school, his father had above average means because he ginned so much cotton, he comes to school in a big eight-thousand-dollar limousine. Harvard and Yale and other schools are bidding on him, offering him academic scholarships to try to get his brain in their school. But this young man is not qualified to go to the local academy here."

"Why?" my son asked.

"Because he's black."

"Well, daddy, that's the only thing about his life that he can't help."

So I got me a new definition there of being prejudiced. A prejudice is having your mind so made up that facts won't change it. Another definition is to discriminate against an individual for something he can't help. This young man had all it took to make a fantastic student at the local private school—money, intelligence, personal appearance, and personality. But they said, "You can't come."

How can you have a school and walk around bragging about it as a quality school, and you've got it in a Christian church, but say it's only for white Christians? A lot of my friends have their children in the all-white academies. One of the evidences that confirms I'm a Christian is that I still love them. And I sincerely hope they'll give me the right to my beliefs and continue to love me.

We got to this bridge we had to cross, and my family decided we would do our dead-level best to stay with the public schools and try to make them work. We could not teach our children that they are privileged because they were born white. My family, along with some others, took a stand. With a minimum of problems, it worked, and we have a fine public school in Yazoo City now. When Walter Cronkite sent his cameras to Yazoo City on the tenth anniversary of the Supreme Court decision to integrate schools, he showed Yazoo City as a Deep South town that had complied with the law and made it work.

The moderator of a Boston TV show asked me about my involvement in these matters, and I told him, "The courts ruled that we had to integrate our schools, just like they've ruled in Boston. We did it several years ago. We made it work . . . and it is working. But it was pretty simple for us to know how to do it because we had some good teachers—some people who showed us how to really get it on."

"Oh, who was that?"

"Busloads from Boston, Massachusetts, came to Mississippi to show us how to integrate our schools. Fellow, I'm not trying to be ugly, I want to be decent and do things decently, but I must tell you that I am shocked to get to Boston and see where you haven't done what you came to Mississippi telling us we needed to do. You're not practicing what you preach. I thought that all the information that Mrs. Endicott Peabody and others from Boston was giving us down in Mississippi was based on experiences they had had in doing this in their own home state. I've talked to some people in Boston, and I've never been so shocked in all my life. I certainly want them to know one thing: whatever they do, they'll do without any meddling from me. I won't go up there meddling, or even help pay anybody's way up there to meddle with them. I'm perfectly willing for each individual area to work out its own problems and do like they ought to do."

Some publications pictured me as being too harsh. I fought a war to give everybody the right to do what they want to do, and one of these rights is to what they do with their children and where they send them to school. I had to pray and do some soul searching about my own situation. I came up with the answer that I cannot flatfooted say I love God but I don't love black people or want my children going to school with them.

Although I despise for a man to be a bigot, thank God we live in a country where a man can choose to be one if he wants to. I've noticed that bigots want me to give them the right to be a bigot, but they don't want to give me the right *not* to be one. They want me to give them the right to hate blacks, but they don't want to give me the right to love them if I want to.

I am as opposed to a bigot as anything in the world, but on occasion, as a Christian, I get a worse feeling toward a man who hasn't changed than I did when I was a bigot. The sin may be bigger. I have to still be Christian and reasonable, and reason with folks, and pray with them . . . and love them.

The hypocrisy bothers me. Some of my friends say, "We didn't leave the public schools due to the black people." Yet they won't sign the compliance pledge saying any qualified student can come to the school.

One of the blessings I've received through all this is that I now know beyond any reasonable doubt that there is none of Jerry Clower in God. God is an omnipotent, wonderful, fair, forgiving, beautiful, precious, saving God. There is none of Jerry Clower in him because if there were a drop of me in God, I know some people that I would turn black.

When the blacks boycotted white businesses in Yazoo City in 1969, they continued buying groceries from Deacon Patenotte—a white man who was a member of the NAACP. Our family was one of the few white families that kept buying groceries from Deacon, and when feelings were running high, one man declared that the trouble with Yazoo City was that people like me kept buying from Deacon. I told the man, "Go ahead, call Walter Cronkite on the telephone. Go down there, and as I come out the front door of the store, shoot me. And let Walter focus that camera on the blood and say, 'War veteran, father of four, shot down in a free country trying to buy groceries at the store of his choice.'"

The biggest disappointment I've had in folks who claim to be Christian was when they put one of those all-white academies inside a church that they claimed was Christian. Pastors, preachers, outstanding stewards and elders all saying, "We've got to do something . . . we don't feel like our children can learn in the public schools so we'll build a school that any qualified student can go to." Don't you know that no black kid is going to go? Ninety-nine percent of them don't have the money, and the rest know they'd be ostracized. It's lying to the children.

They say one of the reasons they have these private schools is so they can read the Bible and pray. Do they pray, "Oh, Lord, we thank you that we ain't nothing but white here, and we're so glad that no black child can come, and we thank you for this great blessing you allow us to have"? Can they pray that prayer? No church can have a segregated all-white academy in it to the glory of God and discriminate against one of

God's people. Because whether they like it or not, if the most heinous Black Panther who ever lived gets gloriously saved like Jerry Clower did at the East Fork Baptist Church, and he's born again and gives his heart to Jesus—that Black Panther, the minute he's born into the kingdom of God, becomes every Christian's brother. And there's nothing they can do about it. God fixed it that way. And he says, "I'm saved, I'm a Christian, I want to go to your Christian school."

"You can't come here because you're black."

And they call it a *Christian* academy. This is against the principles of my upbringing and my Christian principles. It's non-Christian—and God's going to bust their hide.

One statement I made resulted in hundreds of letters—most of them anonymous, and just about all of them contained Citizens Council literature. One anonymous letter from the Ku Klux Klan had eyes drawn on a sheet of paper, and written on the bottom of the page was: "The eyes of the Ku Klux are watching you."

The statement came when I was having lunch with a Jackson sports writer, Larry Guest, and expressed how hurt I was that when school integration came we had some public school coaches who would teach their young men to overcome adversities and how to play when hurt and how to block somebody bigger than you, but when a little rain fell in their life—the rain of integration—they ran. They wouldn't stay in the public schools. And if we're going to save public schools, we have got to have some good leadership to stay. And I named three of the finest coaches in Mississippi who I thought had great leadership—and I was real shocked that they had run.

When that hit the paper, I've never seen so much hate exhibited in people in all my life. This is something I pray about every day. I don't see how in the world that folks could become so emotionally involved in a situation that they can't discuss it intelligently. This is what happened when schools were first integrated. Some folks went all to pieces and couldn't even sit down and discuss it. They could discuss any subject but this. I was alarmed to know some folks who didn't care what time their kids came in at night, or if they were at a beer joint drinking beer, or driving fast on the highway, and they didn't take their children to Sunday school and church, never read the Bible to them, never prayed with them—but the minute they were told their children were going to have to go to school with some blacks, why they exhibited some deep concern. But all these other things were of more concern.

A lady told me, "I've just called the college and found out some information that really thrills me."

"What did you find out?"

"I found out my son is going to be rooming with a white boy next year—and I wasn't going to let him go to that school if he had to room with a Negro."

"Did you find out if his roommate is using dope? If he's smoking marijuana? If he sneaks promiscuous girls into the dormitory room at night? Whether he keeps alcoholic beverages in the room all the time? Or—"

"No. I didn't ask those questions."

"I want you to know here and now I'd rather for my son to room with a born-again black Christian young man than to room with one that's not a Christian that's lily-white."

I'm for truth, whatever the truth is. This is a touchy subject and a lot of folks don't want to discuss it intelligently. I even heard a Baptist deacon say he'd die and go to hell before he'd call a black man "Mister." There's no way . . . no way . . . I can express how opposed I am to that kind of statement.

They were going to have a Jerry Clower Day in Amite County, and some folks blocked it because I didn't send my kids to a private school. Later, however, I was invited to speak to the Amite County Farm Bureau and they called it Jerry Clower Day. It was the largest crowd they ever had.

I don't' hate *anybody*. I love *everybody*. But it alarms me to hear people say, "If you keep our children altogether white, then their morals will be so much better." Some all-white groups have come to me and counseled with me that they have a problem of smoking marijuana or a young lady and a young man had serious moral problems. I don't know who-ever started that lie—I reckon it was Satan—that if you keep everything white, then you won't have any problems about morals.

I've got a long way to go, and I'm still working on my prejudices. It's hard for me to love sissy men. I have to pray about it. But everybody is prejudiced. Every time you change your mind, you rearrange your prejudices.

But what progress we have made! It's just unbeliev-able. I'm so proud of Mississippi. We've made more progress in the last ten years than any other state in the Union. I believe that from the bottom of my heart. I love this state, and I hope we continue to make progress.

I could tell some things that happened when I was a little boy that were appalling and shocking, but those days are gone. And they're not happening now, praise God. Nothing could be accomplished by me getting on national television and knocking things that used to happen. Some of my black friends ought to learn how to forgive and forget. The Lord is not interested in what you used to do but what you're going to do from today on. And I'm wanting to get it on.

7

Reading Jerry's Mail

Do I GET letters! Every day a whole bunch of letters arrives from all kinds of people all over the world. They come to me in Yazoo City, to Rt. 4, Liberty, Mississippi, to my box at the Grand Ole Opry, and to my office at Mississippi Chemical. Every piece of mail I get is acknowledged.

Since most are so complimentary toward me, I didn't pick out the following letters for publication myself. My co-writer, Gerry Wood, selected the letters he thought were most interesting. He said my fans would enjoy reading my mail. All I can say is, I hope you enjoy it half as much as I do.

Dear Jerry,

There are powerfully few people who can stand in front of a bunch of high-school students for one hour and forty-five minutes and have them as interested at the end as at the beginning. But you did!!

We appreciate your time, your interest, and,

most of all, the *kind* of person you are. Kids need people they can admire, and we are lucky to have such as you within touchin' distance.

Sincerely,
Harriet DeCell

Hello Jerry,

We have a son that is confined to bed. He has Muscular Dystrophy and he's on a respirator. He will soon be twenty-four years old. The doctors thought that he wouldn't live this long, but somehow God has spared his life with us and we are thankful. *He loves to hear you talk.* . . . You are one of his favorite people.

Thank you again,

Dear Mr. Clower,

I'm writing you in behalf of our wonderful state. It is very heavy on my heart to urge you to run for governor of Mississippi.

I'm not a politician—just a used-car dealer—but I know the need of God-fearing leaders such as you to lead our state.

I . . . ask you to give this great consideration with your knowledge, your interest in our state, that you have shown so many times and your standards for living, there is no doubt in my mind that you could be elected.

I'm not alone in this. We of North Mississippi will support you all the way.

Vernon Y. Davis

Dear Mr. Clower,

Do you have any puppy's like nicky for sale or do you know any body that has a dog like nicky that might sale one of them it does not matter if one is a female or male if you have one or donot have one write back.

Thank you.

Dear Jerry,

I'm thanking you for the lovely Bible. As you know, I have been traveling and we just started shooting the fourth season of the "Daniel Boone" show, so I have really been hopping.

I too enjoyed our visit—I meet so many nice people every time I travel. I agree with you that the game of life is best played by those who abide by the rules of good conduct.

Thanks again for the "rulebook."

Cordially,
Fess Parker

Dear Mr. Clower,

Your talk and the personal message to my son, Ricky, and the men of the U.S.S. *Enterprise,* have been sent to them, wherever they are in the Indian Ocean, and I know that they will all be tickled to death. Your taking time to send them a private note certainly was above and beyond the call of duty.

Most sincere wishes,
Grover C. Murchison

Dear Jerry,

I felt a desire to write you . . . simply to say "Thank you" for all the nice things you have done for me and all you have meant to me during this and past years. Outside of your dearest loved ones, I do not believe there is another human being who is as proud and thankful for your success as I am. I do not, by any stretch of the imagination, believe it was accidental. I prefer to still believe that God works in mysterious ways his wonders to perform. This just happens to have been his way of putting some extra money into the hands of one of the most generous persons I have ever known.

Sincerely,
Charles J. Jackson

Dear Jerry,

Tandy Rice and I had lunch together today and it was like the James Robertson Parkway Chapter of the Jerry Clower Fan Club, Inc.!

But he worries about you.

Mainly about your agonizing over people who don't understand why you can't accept their particular invitation to speak and entertain, mostly for free. He outlined the procedure which he follows in these cases and it sounded reasonable and right to me. Let him handle all those invitations and get a lot of these people off your back. He can do it diplomatically and save you a lot of grief and unnecessary worry.

I know there is something within your good nature (probably Homerline's influence) to say yes to every good cause and all your old friends. You are just a natch'l born good Samaritan. And I would guess that big old dogs are always licking your hands!

But there is a limit!

In different ways and at a different level, missionaries, popular pulpiteers, golden-voiced denominational workers, movie people, long gangly basketball players and Grand Ole Opry stars have to draw the line somewhere. You are there, my friend! You are going to have to become more philosophical about this business and realize that not everybody is going to understand, but that's *their* problem.

Owen Cooper told me one time that if I ever had any free time I would have to plan it, nobody else would do that for me. If you've got family time or free time or loafing time built into your schedule, that is one of your big "calendar events." There are all kinds of reasons for you feeling absolutely free and justified in holding in reserve some time that you can call your own.

Becky graduated from high school Monday which is a reminder that your kids too will grow up before you know it and be gone. Schedule some of that time for them.

Here endeth the reading of the lesson!

Cordially,
W. C. Fields
Southern Baptist Convention

Dear Jerry,

When I walked in the office this morning I saw a sign which I'm sure you have seen in other business establishments saying that we sometimes forget to say thanks. That sign made me think, Jerry, that I have forgotten to let you know how very much knowing you has meant in my life.

I am once again privileged to be working here and, to a very large degree, I have you to thank for the fact that I have been given a second opportunity in my lifetime to make it to the top. During the time that I was away from this company I had a great deal of time to think about myself, my life-style, my mistakes, my family, and my future. As I thought about these things I constantly found myself thinking about you and your life-style, and how obviously happy you are living a kind of life which is the exact opposite of the life I had been living. These thoughts of you helped me to make a decision which was long overdue; a decision which has changed the course of my life and has brought great happiness not only to me but to those people who care about me the most. I am now able to walk into church on Sunday morning with my wife and boys and take a seat right on the front row without feeling hypocritical or ashamed. My family occupies the place of importance in my life to which they were always entitled but I had failed to give them. In other words, Jerry, I'm on my way to becoming the man I always should have been.

Now I know that with your strong Christian convictions you will say that it was not any human power that changed me and I would not presume to argue any theology with anybody. However, I just want you to know that it was and is the privilege of knowing you and realizing in the dark days that I had met a big man with a big heart who was truly happy living a life different from anything I had ever known that brought me back to where I am now.

If you are ever in this area again I want to invite you into my home so that I can shake your hand and tell you some of these things in person. And this time I guarantee you that I will be there with my wife and family to welcome you into a home that is now a place of happiness largely because of your influence on me and the changes that influence has made in my life.

There is, of course, no way that I can ever really express all of my feelings but I hope this letter at least gives you some idea of the way I feel. I thank you, and I hope that some day, some way I can return the favor.

Sincerely,

Dear Beautiful Jerry,

You are a living, breathing, loving doll and I will never, ever be able to thank you enough as long as I live! I just came back and found that outrageous picture of Elton John. Momma said that your word was worth its weight in gold and I'll never doubt her again—never! You really didn't have to go to all that trouble, though. I'm awfully glad and grateful that you did, but you really didn't have to. I would have understood if you hadn't. You really are too busy a person to go around making silly teenage girls deliriously happy, but I love you for it. . . . Granny and Granddaddy send love—along with my own. Thanks forever & ever!

Becky Calk

Dear Jerry,

It was fun meeting you and working with you. I must confess it bothers me a lot that you cook Butter Beans better than I sing 'em. But I'm practicing.

The enclosed photo is a toothsome twosome if I ever saw one—I hope you like it.

Thanks for my award. A fringe benefit just occurred to me. Doesn't this make me Cousin Dinah?

Dinah Shore

Dear Mr. Clower,

I received your post card last Saturday. I really enjoyed reading it. I also enjoyed your show. . . . When I told everyone I talked to you some people doubted me. But when I show your post card they will believe it. . . . I told the joke today about Marsell's talking chain saw. The kids got a kick out of it.

Your friend always,
Jimmy Hollis

P.S. Mr. Clower,

Jimmy did this nice letter for his writing lesson today. I thought he did a good job. Enjoyed your show, too.

Jimmy's teacher,
Lynda Shaw

Dear Jerry Clower,

You are in my prayers of Thanksgiving for one of God's faithful servants. Yours is an effective ministry. I will always be grateful for your presence at my installation in Washington.

My best to you and Mama and Yazoo friends.

Faithfully,
Jack Allin
Presiding Bishop, Episcopal Church

Dear Jerry,

I want to say "Thank you" for the gift of sending my son to seminary. This could not have been accomplished had you not contributed to send him. From the bottom of my heart, I thank you and ask God to bless you always.

Also, thank you for the guidance and advice you have given him all through the years since he was called to preach the gospel. You helped in so many ways and for this, I thank God for you.

Gratefully yours,

Dear Mr. Clower,

It is quite refreshing and pleasurable to know there is someone in the vicinity who has more than a passing interest in the state, its change, and hopefully its progress in the area of race relations and all it brings.

That is an area that is much more easily ignored than coped with by many people I have come in contact with here. I sincerely hope there are more people like you in the state because only through the efforts and dedication of such people will the causes that have been won be maintained and a beginning for other progress established.

Sincerely,
Joe Stebbins
The *Clarion-Ledger* and Jackson,
Mississippi, *Daily News*

Dear Jerry,

I want you to know how much I enjoyed the time we spent together in El Paso and on the plane from Atlanta to Tampa.

I strongly suspect that good things will continue to come your way, and, as we say in my native Tennessee, "it pleasures me."

All the best.

Sincerely,
Lindsey Nelson

Dear Sir:

My name is Lori Bryan. I am 8 years old. I am in the 3rd grade and am in my 1st year of 4-H. I have a steer named Marcel who is a one year old. He is a pretty steer. He is angus X. He wants to go his own way at times. But I'm working hard with him. Would you please bid on him for me. I would be very happy if you would. Then I will be able to pay my feed bill. I will be showing at the youth fair. I'm going to use my left over money to go to college.

Sincerely,
Lori Bryan

8

What Am I?

JUST ABOUT EVERYWHERE I go somebody will ask, "Jerry, what are you?"

"I am a Christian."

"Yeah, but what *are* you?"

"I am a Christian and I worship in a Southern Baptist church. The denomination I belong to is Southern Baptist, but I want to impress upon everybody that I am more Christian than I am Baptist. If you find an individual who is more Baptist than he is Christian, you'd better watch him because he won't do."

People should get off in a quiet place and review a few things in their lives. If I could gather up everybody in the whole world and preach a sermon as a Baptist layman and as a Christian entertainer, here is what I would do.

First, I would make for sure that I was saved. I would. A dear man who belonged to another church told me I was very presumptuous and braggadocio to have the audacity to say that I know I was saved. Well,

I know who my daddy was, I know who my wife is. I know a lot of things; so consequently I ought to know whether I'm saved or not. The Apostle Paul in the Bible knew. Not only did Paul say he knew he was saved, but he said he knew he was saved forever. And I believe that too. If a man is genuinely converted, if he becomes a child of God, then he couldn't break into hell if he tried. That's just the way it works.

After I made sure that I was saved, I would seek out a New Testament Bible-believing church, put my membership in that church, and make them a good hand. An individual can do better in a church than he can do out. When I was a little boy, my mother would say, "Son, you don't have to say 'church house' any more than you say tooth dentist or neck tie." When you say the church, you certainly aren't talking about the church house.

But in a way I was right. The church is where the signals are called every Sunday. The preacher is the quarterback, and he gets up and calls the plays. Then you leave the church house to take the church out into the world and use it that coming week. The next Wednesday night or Sunday you come back and get your battery all charged up again. You can run the plays without coming down to the church house and hearing what the plays are, but you can't run them right. You'll block the wrong fellow just like a tackle in a football game—if he doesn't know what play they're running, he may block somebody into the play. This is what a lot of folks do who claim they can do as well at home and don't ever come to church. Sometimes they say, "I was down there in spirit." Well, I don't believe in ghosts, never have believed in them, and ain't going to start believing in them now.

I would be faithful to the church and go even on Sunday night. If I didn't go on Sunday night, I would go to the next business meeting and make a motion that we call off preaching on Sunday night. My reason for doing this would be that I wouldn't want any of my friends subjected to something down at the church house on Sunday night that I didn't believe in enough to ever go to. What would happen, though, if you made that motion, especially in a Baptist church like I go to, is that the folks who never come on Sunday night would show up the day that you voted, and they would vote to keep having church where them folks what's been coming could keep coming and them what's been staying at home will stay at home.

Then I would tithe my income. My local church could depend on me to give at least 10 percent of my salary every month. Some people say it's easy for me to do this because I'm in show business and make a lot of money. But I tithed my income before I ever got into show business. I tithed my check as a fertilizer peddler. There are a lot of things that are suggested I do in the word of God that are hard for me to do. But I can come as near in my giving to doing what the Lord wants me to do as anything else in my Christian life. If anybody would try this who hasn't tried it, and it doesn't work and God doesn't bless them, I'll probably write another book and apologize and tell them I didn't know what I was talking about.

You can't outgive God. If folks who claim to be Christian would all start tithing income, there would never be another cake walk, Bingo game, rummage sale, or spaghetti supper because folks who love God would dip down into their pockets and give back a portion of what he's blessed them with, and they'd cut out all this stuff. My church has so many tithers that they don't need rummage sales or women baking cakes. I feel like that cheapens the cause of Christ—but I don't have any argument with folks who do it. I asked some folks in another church why didn't they just raise the money and give it, and they said the women love to get together to make those cakes and sell them—it gives them a period of fellowship. That reminds me of my wife back when I made the salary of a fertilizer salesman: she used to talk about how she loved to sew, how she enjoyed making all the dresses for our little girls. It's kind of ironic that since I'm no longer on the salary scale of a fertilizer salesman, she very seldom ever sews.

It's also important not to be a nit-picker. I wouldn't care what color shirt the preacher wore—it doesn't make any difference. If you go to church to find fault and want to nit-pick about what they're doing down there, I would suggest that you go to the church office and pick up a visitation card and go visit the family listed on that card. Open your Bible, look them in the eye, and win them to the Lord. The Sunday this family comes to publicly profess their faith in Christ and join your church . . . wooo, man! . . . your heart will be so thrilled that 99 and 44/100 percent of your nit-picking would be over. You'd be so thrilled doing what God wanted you to do, you wouldn't have time to nit-pick.

Next, you should spend as much time trying to get some people to come to your church as you do making sure some people don't come. I hope this is not confusing. Unfortunately, some churches actually appointed committees to draw up a plan to keep certain folks from coming to the church. The preacher occasionally would preach, "Whosoever will, may come," and during the invitation he would say, "Everybody ought to be saved and come on down the aisle and get your heart right with the Lord." But that was just the folks they allowed to come inside the church house.

The reason I can praise God and go right on after I see injustices done is that I smile and say, "Lord, you're going to handle that, and I'm leaving it up to you so ol' Jerry ain't going to worry about it." In case you're still confused and don't know what I mean: I'm talking about some churches make certain that no blacks ever come. Whoever shows up at the church house ought to be allowed to come in and worship the Lord God.

In some instances I can see where folks ought to visit any family and win them to Jesus. We don't proselytize now if there's a family that's already in a church different from mine. We don't bang on their door and say, "You oughta come over to our church —we know you ain't enjoying where you're going." Instead, we take church surveys and try to see who's unchurched, and win them. You've got to be wise as a serpent and harmless as a dove.

To give you a perfect illustration, I belong, in my opinion, to the finest Southern Baptist church in all of the world. My church comes as near doing what God wants a church to do—on missions, giving, and leadership—as any church in the Southern Baptist Convention. I'm so thankful to God that I'm a member of the First Baptist Church of Yazoo City, Mississippi, because when I have a burden I want to go to the middle of the church house and tell all the folks who make up the church that I have a burden and please pray for me. That's what the Scripture says: "Bear ye one another's burdens and so fulfill the law of Christ."

Not too long ago our church invited the choir of Mississippi College to come and sing. A few weeks before the choir was to arrive someone from the college called the church. "We want to let you know that when you invited this choir we didn't have a black in the choir, but now we've got one. Out of ninety-four students, one of them is black, and if the choir comes, we're bringing them all."

This was brought up before the deacons, discussed, and brought to a Sunday morning vote. Here's another reason why I'm a Southern Baptist. Each church is autonomous. Regardless of what you want to do in a Southern Baptist church, the people get up and express themselves. Then we vote—and that's the way it is. My thirteen-year-old daughter has got the same vote as the preacher. Nobody runs a Southern Baptist church except the people. It's one of the true real democracies left in the whole world. It was voted by a majority to let the choir come on with the one black student.

This is one of the greatest tests I've had of being a Christian and reacting like one. My own Sunday school teacher got up—and not only did he vote that the young man couldn't come, but he was trying to be on both sides by saying, "Just because you vote that this choir can't come ain't no sign that you hate somebody." That somewhat bothered me. In fact I decided I wasn't ever going back to Sunday school any more if he taught the class. When I got home and got down on my knees and prayed about it, I decided this was the wrong thing to do. I love my Sunday school teacher very much, and I have rich sweet fellowship every time I go to Sunday school. So I have continued to go.

I'll tell you one thing: I saw people there that morning that I hadn't seen in my church in years and years and years. So if you want to get a big attendance in your church, maybe you ought to start up a ruckus. These people will stand before God. Here is a man or a woman who doesn't come to church, or invite anybody else to come—and the only time they would ever decide to come to church was the day they had the right to vote to make sure somebody else couldn't come. Does that make any sense as a Christian? Does it make any sense at all?

The choir came. The folks who voted for the young man not to come showed up. The spirit about it was beautiful. And it proved that you can have a discussion —everybody have their say, decently and in order— vote, and let the majority run it. I was a little concerned about one or two of my friends who voted against the choir coming. They had been telling me, "If some of these black people would just try to do a better job —if they'd just try to make something out of themselves, then I would have more respect for them." Well, here is a young man who is making something out of himself, who's going to a fine Christian college, who not only is excelling by being there but he tried out for the traveling choir and got up and did the "Do-re-me-fa-so-la-ti-do" in competition with others, and won. He did it so good and he tried to amount to something so good that he even won out over some white folks. Here's one who tried to make something out of himself, and some of the people *still* voted that he couldn't sing in their church.

If I were God, I would have set me up one of those deals in the back of the church house like they've got at the airport—when you walk through that thing at the airport with a metal object on you, ZEEEOOO! they'll stop you and search you. I'd set me up a rig in the church, and when an individual showed up at his church for the first time in years and the only reason he was coming was to vote to keep someone else from coming, when his foot passed over the threshold and my divine indicator sounded off, ZEEEOOO! he would be black when he broke that barrier. If I were God, that's the way I'd do it. Thank God, I ain't God, and he ain't letting me run it, but in the event he ever does, I'm keeping me a list of folks. . . .

If we polled all the pastors in the world and asked them what was the biggest disappointment they have had in their ministry, it would probably be in folks who claimed to be Christian, but when something came up they went all to pieces and acted like pagans. Many things happen in my life that I see other people get so excited about. They can hardly stand it—they bite their fingernails, and cry, "My soul, what in the world's going to happen?"

Christian folks ought to act like Christians, and pagan folks ought to act like pagans. I have seen people I thought were good strong stable Christians with a deep faith, and a little rain fell in their life and they went to pieces. They didn't lean on God. Like some folks when they lose a loved one. They're going to be sad because they're going to be lonely, but if I believe anything the Bible says I believe what it says about the hereafter. There are some things worse than dying. One man lost his wife and it took three or four folks to keep him from getting in the grave with her. "I've lost her—my life is ruined! There ain't no hope for me. I just can't stand it—I'll never look at another woman." He's a big Baptist churchgoer, and in three months he has remarried. So how did that impress the young people standing at the grave site?

I pray every day that if I'm ever thrown in the fire, I will be found faithful.

The closest that God ever came to throwing me in the fire was Friday before Mother's Day in 1970. We had gone to bed, and the phone rang. My Amy answered it. "Daddy, there's a lady on the telephone and she wants to talk to you and it's near about midnight."

"Well, darling, maybe the lady has got the wrong number."

I went to the telephone and this lady said, "This is Mrs. Bridgforth out in the county." I knew who the lady was—a very prominent Yazoo County family. "My daughter was having a spend-the-night party and your son and three more boys from Yazoo City were out here visiting. At 11:30, your son announced that he was required to be home by twelve o'clock and he had to leave. The boys left—and down at the foot of the hill here in front of my house are some barriers where some road construction is going on, and the boys missed the turn. They've had a wreck. The two boys on the front seat are all right. But your son and one more boy on the back seat . . . the one boy is cut up and, Mr. Clower, I'm sorry to tell you, but your son is out and we cannot wake him up." I thought this meant that my son was dead.

"Well, Mrs. Bridgforth, let me get some britches on and I'll be out there immediately, and I sincerely thank you for calling me."

"The ambulance has been called and they're on their way out here now. You may meet the ambulance coming back on your way out here."

I put my clothes on, cranked the car, and told my wife what had happened and that she'd better call Marguerite Hill to stay with Katy who was three weeks old and for her to meet me at the hospital or be there when the ambulance came in.

While driving out to the scene of the accident to-

ward Benton, Mississippi, I started praying. "Lord, I
have been all over this country, popping off about
what I ought to do if tragedy hits my life—that I
shouldn't react like a pagan, I ought to react like a
Christian. Lord, I want you to know that I have
believed everything I have ever said about if I am
thrown in the fire to be found faithful. And, Lord, I
also want you to know that every morning of my life
I get up and say my prayer to you. Now, Lord, it's
hard—it's not easy for me to do this—but I want
you to know that when I get out to the scene of that
wreck, if my boy is dead, I'm going to praise your
holy name. If my boy is alive, I'm going to praise
your holy name. You have never made a mistake, you
ain't going to make one with me. I am on your side. To
God be the glory."

Right then I didn't know what I was going to find
at the scene of the wreck. But I had peace in my heart
that I had prayed the right prayer to stand whatever
would be put on me. About a mile from the accident I
met the ambulance. At the scene of the wreck I let the
window down and thanked Mrs. Bridgforth and others
who helped.

"Mr. Clower, we can't wake your boy up. He's on
the way to the hospital." So I followed the ambulance
back into town and when I got to the hospital, there
stood my dear friend Chief Hill standing over my son
with Dr. John Chapman, my family doctor.

Dr. Chapman looked up at me. "Your son is alive.
He's knocked out. I don't seem to know what happened. It looks like there's a soft spot right on the top
of his head, and he's out, and all we can do is watch
him."

We checked him into a room, and we stood there
and watched him. Teen-agers came and sat down along
the hallways all over the hospital. And people were
praying.

The next morning, Dr. Chapman came back and
checked him. "He should have responded by now.

We're going to have to send him to Jackson to a brain specialist."

Well, folks, I had to do some praying. I stood over my son and I broke down. I started crying.

But I also prayed. "Lord, I don't understand all this, but I want you to know I'm on your side, and you are powerful enough to use this to your glory."

They rolled a little table in there and put him on it. I walked out and got in the ambulance. Emergency. The siren started. And to Jackson we went. As we were going down Grand Avenue in Yazoo City, I saw friends of mine stopping on the street. Service station attendants stopping the gas from running, and bowing their heads and praying for me and praying for my boy.

When we got to the emergency room at Jackson, some of the finest specialists in the country were standing there. They examined my son and had the same report as Dr. Chapman. "No pressure has built up—but he's down here where we can watch him, and the minute pressure builds up we may have to do something." They put him in intensive care, and we were not allowed to see him except five minutes on the hour. We sat down in the intensive care waiting room.

Now, folks, if you think you've got problems, you ought to go visit the intensive care waiting room at your local hospital. You'll have your eyes opened, and you'll see what you thought were problems ain't nothing.

The phone rang, and it was Dr. Chapman calling from Yazoo City. "Big man, I want to tell you like it is. Some pressure could start building up on your boy, and if it does, they got to go in there, operate, bore a hole in his skull. And I wanted him down there where some folks who really know how to do this can do it."

For three days and nights my wife and I, and several of our friends, would come and go. One dear friend, Mrs. Sidney Holley—the Holleys were fine Methodist people who live in Jackson now—came to the hospital, sat down in the waiting room, and declared, "I ain't leaving until I know something about Ray."

Beautiful. Ain't it great to have friends? All during this, my pastor, other preachers, and Christian friends would come to see us. In the meantime, my Gideon buddies had been calling one another, and they had been praying. The phone rang about an hour later, and it was Jack Stack from Meridian, Mississippi—a very wealthy oil man and a very dear Christian friend of mine. "Jerry, don't worry about anything. I don't know what's going to happen, but I have prayed and I have perfect peace in my heart that God is going to use this to his glory. And are you willing to accept whatever happens?"

"Jack, I've turned it over to the Lord. Me and my wife are praying about it, and we said, 'God, he belongs to you—whatever you want to do, you do it, and we're going to praise your holy name.'"

My son didn't say one word or draw a conscious breath, and it killed me to go in there and look down in his face—a big two-hundred-pound boy, built like Tarzan, a good high-school football player, and he didn't say a word to his daddy or his mama.

Three days later, Dr. Hodges walked into intensive care, examined him, and said, "Get Ray Clower out of here and put him in a private room and feed him. He's going to be all right."

And not only was he all right, but he played football the next year. Ultimately he went on to a junior college where he made all-state, and never had a speck of trouble with his head. To God be the glory—great things he has done.

Likewise, never underestimate the power of Satan. There is a devil, he is real, and he does go around like a roaring lion trying to devour folks. I have seen some foot slipping going on in my own church that I knew couldn't happen. I need to pray first thing every morning, to read my Bible every day, to go hear a sermon every Sunday, to go to prayer Wednesday night if at

(Gerry Wood photo)
Jerry points to the baptizing
hole near the East Fork Baptist
Church where he and Homerline were
baptized.

The East Fork Baptist Church.

Noontime at Babe's and Big Mama's house.

(Gerry Wood photo)

Jerry with his folks, Mr. and Mrs. Elliott Moore—"Babe" and "Big Mama."

Bill (Sonny) and Jodie Clower show their travel trailer to Jerry.

(Gerry Wood photo)

Sonny tells a good one to Jodie and Jerry.

The Clower Boys: Jerry (left) and Sonny.

The Rogues of Route Four. That's Jerry third from the right, and Sonny second from the right.

The graduating class at East Fork High, 1944. That's Jerry in the front row, right. In the back row next to Ardel is Raynell. She didn't have on her cap and gown, so she hid behind Ardel.

Navy days.

Homerline and Jerry back in the courting days.

Jerry Clower ready for the snap at Mississippi State in 1949.

(Gerald Crawford photo courtesy Southern Living *Magazine)*
Ol' 77 has some advice for new 77. Jerry confers with his
son Ray during Ray's football career at Holmes Junior
College.

(Gerry Wood photo)

Little Katy "sneaked up" on me and Mama!

At home a few years back with (left to right) Sue, Katy, Amy, and Homerline.

Daddy Jerry visits Amy and her husband Billy Elmore.

Amy at the piano.

The pride of Mississippi Chemical.

Jerry with his super-secretary at Mississippi Chemical, Judy Moore.

Jerry behind his desk at Mississippi Chemical Corporation.

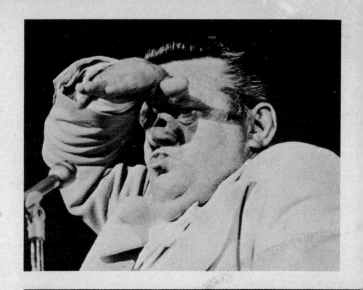

(WSM photo by Les Leverett)
Jerry entertains a record-breaking Grand Ole Opry crowd of 6,000 the night in 1975 when floodwaters forced the Opry out of Opryland and into Municipal Auditorium.

Governor William Waller of Mississippi congratulates Jerry on his induction into the Grand Ole Opry.

Jerry talks with his producer, Snuffy Miller, as Charlie Douglas of WWL, New Orleans, looks on.

Jerry recording "live" in Picayune, Mississippi.

Jerry with Dinah Shore.

Jerry Clower "demolishes" Jimmy Dean on

"The Jimmy Dean Show."

Jerry Clower and Jerry Wallace on "The Johnny Bench Show."

David Frost and Debbie Reynolds get a chuckle out of a Clower comment on "The David Frost Show."

(Michael G. Borum photo)

The Oak Ridge Boys, Charley Pride, and Jerry Clower.

Two music business heavies: Kenny Price and Jerry Clower on the set of CBS-TV's "Orange Blossom Special."

(Michael G. Borum photo)

(Hope Powell photo)

Bless his heart! Jerry with Freddy Hart.

"Up beside Loretta Lynn, I am a city slicker."

Clower meets Kojak. Jerry and actor Telly Savalas at Universal Studios, Hollywood, California.

Nashville journeys to Yazoo City as Tandy Rice signs Jerry to his Top Billing Agency.

Tandy Rice, president of Top Billing Agency and Jerry's personal manager; Barbara Farnsworth of Top Billing; and Jerry.

"The greatest all-around moral Christian gentleman I've ever known is Owen Cooper."

Jerry with his pastor, Jim Yates.

"If they were going to shoot one of us, I'd tell them to shoot me, but to make sure that when the bullet hit me it didn't ricochet and hurt Charles J. Jackson in any way."

Jerry and his "Country Consultant"—Chief Carey Hill.

Milking rattlesnakes in Sweetwater, Texas.

Jerry walks the "high ground" where Pa Homer and many of the characters in his stories are buried.

all possible, and, after all of this, to read the Word of God and pray to overcome temptation. I need this to try to stay strong enough to overcome temptation. The devil has an alphabetical list of my temptations—he knows what will tempt me, and I need to be strong in the Lord to overcome these temptations. I have seen deacons in churches who have been with their wife and family for years and years when Satan put temptation in their path—and they didn't overcome the temptation, and it wrecked homes and caused trouble. Satan will do it to anybody. He's no respecter of persons.

That ends the sermon I would preach to everybody if I had the opportunity to do it. Everybody ought to be saved, be a member of a New Testament Bible-believing church, be faithful to the church and attend every function they possibly can, they should tithe their income, they ought not to be a nit-picker, they should make certain that they spend as much time trying to get people in the church as they do trying to keep some people out, they ought to act like Christians—not pagans—if tragedy hits their life, and they ought not to underestimate the power of Satan—he is powerful.

The church is where it's at. The first place of Christian service for any Christian is in a local church. I walked into church one morning and a lady ran up to me, grabbed me, hugged me, screamed, and started crying with joy.

"Mrs. Johnson, what in the world is going on?"

"I just got a letter from my son, and he was looking through the albums at the P.X. in Saigon, Vietnam. And there was your album, 'Mouth of Mississippi,' with a picture of you. And he screamed. The people ran over and asked what was the matter, and he said, 'That man taught me in Sunday school. That's Mr. Jerry Clower, and he's from Yazoo City, Mississippi.' He got the album and played it after he came in from a patrol where a lot of them had been shot up. They got to where they would come in from patrol and, without discussing the losses—it was just automatic—they'd put the album on and get into it. It was something they could do to help forget about the tragic shooting, killing, and squalor."

You've got to be strong. One day my secretary notified me that the wife of a friend of mine in Monroeville, Alabama, had died. I got him on the phone and told him, "I'm not calling to tell you I know how you feel, and I'm sure a lot of people have rushed up to you and said 'Oh, I know how you feel,' but unless they've had a young wife to die with cancer and left them with several children they don't have any idea how you feel. So I'm not calling you to say I know how you feel because I don't. But I do know this. God ain't going to put no more on you than you can stand. I am on your side. And there are a lot of things worse than dying. I'm just going to tell you I love you. And the Bible says, 'Bear ye one another's burdens and so fulfill the law of Christ.' I'm calling to tell you that I'm helping to bear your burdens."

"Thank you, Jerry."

9

Home, Sweet Christian Home

A CHRISTIAN HOME is a place where every member of the family is in love with the Lord—and they all act like it.

The person with the greatest responsibility for a Christian home is that individual called daddy. God lets us reproduce—and the human being doesn't have any natural urges that God hasn't so planned for that urge to be satisfied decently, clean, and in a manner that is morally right. If a man satisfies his urges in a manner other than how God has laid it out to be satisfied, then it's filthy sin.

What a responsibility to be a daddy! But, my, how wonderful it is to live in a house where the woman who loves you is a fine Christian. And children who love you and your wife, watch your every move, and literally mimic you. How can your responsibility be any greater than to set the proper example in the home?

The greatest mistake made in our society today is for daddy to take the attitude that his child is being trained and disciplined in the school and church. That simply ain't so. We have four children. I have a son, Ray; a daughter, Amy; a daughter, Sue; and a daughter, Katy. The most sincere age of any individual is when they're a child. How you impress children will be as important an impression as will ever be made on their lives.

The sincerity of a child—my soul! I marvel at how sincere they are when they say their blessing. My children ask, "Daddy, tell us the coon hunting story." I reckon I've told it a jillion times in my house—and every time after I tell the story, there's a different question asked: a sincere question about something that happened.

A former pastor of mine, Rev. Harold Shirley, a long tall gospel-preaching preacher whom I love dearly, was visiting in my home one Sunday night after church. We opened up a few cans of sardines, got out some of that old hoop cheese that I used to eat down at Rt. 4, Liberty, Mississippi, had a period of fellowship and fun, then Brother Shirley and his family went home. It wasn't long until we got a telephone call, and he was laughing so hard he could hardly talk. "Jerry, I got to tell you what our son Ken did while we were having our evening devotion."

After the Shirleys had gotten home, they went to the bedroom, read the Bible, and they were to have the evening prayer. As the Shirleys got on their knees —their daughter Jan Robbin and their little boy Ken —they started a prayer. Brother Shirley prayed, Mrs. Shirley prayed, then it got to Ken who was four years old. Ken started praying, and since we were good friends of the family, he prayed for the Clower family.

"Dear Lord, God bless Mr. Clower, God bless Ray, God bless Amy, God bless Sue, and God bless . . . ah, God bless—" And he couldn't think of my wife's name. Homerline. He had called her Miss Homerline, but he couldn't think of her then. So he started all over again. "Dear Lord, God bless Mr. Clower, God bless Ray, God bless Amy, God bless Sue, and God bless

. . . ah, God bless——" He still couldn't think of her name. I don't know of any adults who wouldn't have just skipped over Miss Homerline. Frankly, I would have skipped her and prayed, "Lord, I can't remember her name, but I'll sure get her next time."

Ken was struggling. He didn't want to skip this lady, he wanted to pray for her. Brother Shirley raised up and looked at Mrs. Shirley. Ken bowed his head again, and started all over. "Dear Lord, God bless Mr. Clower, God bless Ray, God bless Amy, God bless Sue, and Lord . . . ah . . . ah . . . Lord, please bless that woman what lives with Mr. Clower."

Here is the living example of the sincerity of a child. Ken Shirley wanted to pray for my wife, and he made sure that he included her. From that day to now, the Shirleys refer to my dear wife as "that woman what lives with Mr. Clower."

My Sue, when she was six years old, went with her mother to school one day to pick up Ray. While Sue was sitting in the car outside the school waiting for the bell to ring, a good friend of ours pulled up to get his son. When Sue saw Mr. Tom Raggett drive up, she told her mother she wanted to go over there and visit with him. She was allowed to do this. Mr. Raggett opened the car door and let her in, and it wasn't but a minute until Sue started jabbering and talking. Mr. Raggett opened the car door, got out, and walked back to my wife's car. He was laughing so much that tears were coming down his cheeks. "Homerline, do you know what Sue just told me?"

"There's no telling what Sue just told you."

"When Sue got in my car, I asked her, 'Sue, have you ever heard of Jerry Clower?' And she wheeled around, pointed her finger at my face, and said, 'Why, I've got one!' "

Volumes could be written about Sue's statement. Yes, she has got one. He's her daddy. And her daddy should strive to live each and every day—twenty-four hours a day—the kind of life that she will be proud she has one as long as she lives.

To maintain a Christian home, it's very important to have a family altar or a family worship service sometime during each day. But this is hard to do. You have every kind of schedule in the world—you go here and go there—and it's hard to find a time to get the whole family together. But it should be done, if at all possible. If all the family cannot be together on any particular day, then have a family devotional period with that group you do have present.

Make sure that each member of your family who is old enough to read becomes addicted to reading God's Word, and to praying each and every day of their lives. One of the real thrills is to walk down the hall on the way to bed and see through the door that each one of your children has got the daily Bible readings. They have looked in the Baptist Training Union Quarterly and have found the recommended Bible passage for that day. When a family lives together, prays together, plays together, and literally lives under one roof like all who are in love with the Lord God . . . my, what a wonderful privilege it is to be alive and receive the rich benefits from such a home.

When I started reading the Bible as a child, I did it for the wrong reason—to be a hundred in Training Union. I should have read it because I wanted to hide it in my heart where I wouldn't sin against the Lord. At least I developed a habit of reading it every day. Regardless, there ain't much way to read the Bible wrong like some folks criticize some methods of winning people to the Lord. If you get somebody saved, it's kind of hard for me to understand how you can get somebody converted wrong.

A daddy should not have any bad habits or bad language or other faults children could develop. I don't drink, I don't smoke, I don't cuss, I don't lie, I don't cheat, and I just love one woman. I *am* a hog. My main problem is that I'm too fat. I've lost two thousand pounds in the last ten years. I've got some children that have developed bad eating habits, and if they don't discipline themselves and change, they're going to become hogs, too. If I didn't have to fool with food at all, I wouldn't fool with it. Just like liquor. Even though most of the folks I run with, especially in show business, are social drinkers, there's no temptation for me to drink. I don't have to have it to survive. But you've got to fool with food. I get to fooling with it and I end up eating too much. Record promoters meet me about everywhere I go—and the minute I hit the ground off the airplane, they say, "Man, I've got this new place. I want to take you to eat some ribs." Or a bean place, or corn-on-the-cob place. And every place has a lot of calories.

I don't care what your philosophy of life is, do you reckon there is any daddy in the world who would recommend to his children that they ought to take up smoking? We can develop habits to serve God like we can develop habits to serve the devil.

I never met a young man who was a bigot or a racist, and popped off about it, that his daddy wasn't a bigot also. Sometimes if the parents had let the children settle racial misunderstandings, they would have come out a lot better. I'm leaning toward young folks and can hardly wait to turn this country over to some of them. The young people are so much better now than they were when I was growing up.

While playing football at Mississippi State, we were having a practice scrimmage and Joe Fortunato—a friend of mine and a former all-pro great with the Chicago Bears—had stepped in my face. The doctor put eight stitches above one of my eyes and painted me with a bunch of old red medicine. Not only did I look terrible, I *felt* terrible. I went home to my little veteran's apartment and my wife came out on the porch. She was in deep sympathy with me about how I was hurt, and sorry that I got stepped on.

Someone had had a baby in the community and had given me a cigar. I went to the bedroom and got my cigar out of the chifforobe drawer, sat on the front porch, yelled at my wife to bring me some kind of cold sody water, struck a big kitchen match, and fired up that stogie. I was blowing that smoke and knew if I could smoke that cigar, it'd keep my head from hurting and make me relax. While puffing smoke out through the air, I looked next door and there stood a little boy by the name of Washington. He was standing on the porch coloring in his coloring book. He took the crayon and put it in his mouth, reached up and took it out with two fingers, and he puckered up his mouth like he was blowing smoke out. His daddy came out of the house and looked down at him. "Daddy, I want you to know that you lied to me."

I looked over there right quick. I knew exactly how you were supposed to handle children inasmuch as I didn't have any of my own back then, and I said to myself, "I'd backhand him off the porch—I'd never let a young one tell me I had lied."

"Roy, what do you mean I lied to you?"

"Sure, you lied to me. You told me you couldn't play football if you smoked. Jerry Clower plays football and he's smoking. Look at him."

I didn't know whether to go in the house or under it, but I kept puffing on my free cigar. And Roy did, too. He put the crayon back in his mouth.

"Roy, what in the world are you doing?"

With disgust he stomped the porch and said, "Daddy, can't you see? I'm smoking. Just like Jerry Clower."

I walked over to Roy's front yard. "Roy, I'll quit if you will." And I put that cigar down and took my foot and stomped the end of it out. Roy put down his little crayon and took his foot and stomped the crayon.

All the excuses in the world can be given, but please note here and now, regardless of what others say, I was convinced that I was leading little Roy to do wrong. And, God being my helper, I don't want to lead any child to do any wrong.

The main disciplinarian in the home should be ol' daddy. The Bible says if you bring up a child the way he should go, when he gets old he won't depart from it. Each and every one of my children has been carried out of church, paddled, brought right back into church, and promised faithfully right there that they'd get another good one if they didn't behave. This works. I recommend it.

Please don't lie to your children. I go to the swimming hole with my kids, and some daddy will beg his child for thirty minutes, "Please, darling, please get out of the pool—it's time to go, pretty please, won't you come on home with daddy . . ."

That galls me so bad I try to get my kids to the other end of the swimming hole where I won't see a grown adult man in public lie to his kids. Because if he says, "I'm going to whip you if you don't get out of the pool," and then they don't get out of the pool, he has stood there and told a bald-faced lie. You prove your love for your children if you make them behave more than if you let them misbehave. It just isn't fair to the child.

A good father will sincerely appreciate other people notifying him about one of his children misbehaving. You ought to react in an appreciative manner that shows you are extremely pleased that they would think enough of you to call this to your attention. Some people I dearly love I would hesitate to call if I saw their child drag racing or running a red light or for anything else because I'm convinced they would hate you for the rest of their life, and they'd go all around the country saying you had lied about one of their children.

One day one of our friends who goes to the same church called the house, and this lady told my wife that all day long our son had been calling their little girl on the phone and worrying her. The little girl had said, "Please stop calling." But, she said, our son did not stop calling—in fact, the last two times he called, he said some rather ugly things to this girl. And he was supposed to have told this girl that his name was Ray Clower after saying these ugly things.

My wife said, "I sincerely appreciate you calling. You don't know how much I appreciate you reporting this to me, but tell me, how long have these calls been going on?"

"They started yesterday afternoon, and he's called all day today, and I want you to stop it."

"My son, Ray Clower, is out of town with his daddy, and they've been in St. Louis for the past four days."

Now do you see what happened? The mother and that little girl would have gone through life thinking that our son called and used ugly language had she not loved us enough to call and tell us she thought our child was misbehaving.

The greatest need in America today is for more Christian homes that exemplify proper training and teaching. One of the greatest menaces is the breakdown of a home. I'm the product of a broken home, but I want to hasten to say that the Lord Jesus Christ can mend a broken home and make it stronger after the break than it was before. I get so downhearted listening to some families talk. While I was waiting for a plane at the airport back during the Watergate mess, this handsome couple was talking to their daughter who was going back to college. This mother and father told their child about how awful Watergate was and used it as an illustration about lying and cheating and "My soul, isn't this awful?" and "Those people ought to be put under the jail." As the girl boarded the plane, she turned and hollered at her mother, "When I get to school, I'll call you."

"That's right, darling. Just make a collect call to yourself—and we'll know this is your signal that you're in school and you're all right."

I wanted to vomit. There was a couple telling their child about the damnable Watergate, but had figured out a way to teach her to cheat and lie to the telephone company. Later on they'll criticize their child for lying about something.

At the ticket booth of a big amusement park, I was buying tickets for my children and two of their friends who were twelve. I explained truthfully to the lady the ages of the children and asked how much money she wanted. She told the two little girls, "Just tell everybody you are eleven." I said, "Lady, I'm trying to teach my kids not to lie." And it made the lady mad, she got huffy. She didn't want me to correct her.

Oh, what a shame for a father to let a child go to a picture show and lie about his age to save a few pennies.

Now I'd like to talk about the mother. How wonderful to live with a godly woman who smiles about things, shares things with you that the children said, the things that are funny, the things that can be discussed to cause each of you to use what was said to be a better mother or a better father.

Sometimes when I return from doing a show, I drive up in my car and can't find a parking place around my house. I say "Praise God from whom all blessings flow" because most of the cars brought children to recite the Word of God to my wife. She's in the Bible Memory Association, and these children come by so many times a week to recite portions of God's Word. My wife hears these young people, keeps the record, and sends it off so awards can be given to those who completed memorizing certain amounts of Scripture. Some men when they get home in the afternoon can't find a parking place because the ladies are having a big meeting or planning something for the children to do in the community that might even be a detriment to them.

Children should be children while they are children. I don't appreciate grown adult people—good people —giving parties, and if that type of party is given at all, it certainly should be for adults. When you start children doing adult things, then they want to live like adults, and God forbid we want our children not to be children. When they get old enough to think for themselves, they can decide as free moral agents which way they want to go. Some of the biggest mistakes made in the world are when parents say, "Oh, well, we left it up to our boy . . . he's twelve . . . and he oughta be making the decisions on whether he wants to be going over there or not, or whether he wants to do this or not." Children need counseling, guidance. His Christian daddy should help him make the decisions after discussing it with his Christian mother—and the decision should be best for the child.

On South State Street in Chicago there's a wonderful institution that has helped so many thousands through the years—the Pacific Garden Mission. On the threshold of the mission door are the words: *Mother's prayers follow you.* A truer statement has never been made by anybody anywhere.

As a teen-ager aboard an aircraft carrier in the South Pacific, I was being taught how to kill people. After we'd be under attack with Japanese planes diving on the ship, I would lie in my bunk reading my Testament and praying for God to give me strength. The next day the chaplain would get on the P.A. system while we were under attack, and he'd yell, "There's a plane diving on the Hornet—get down everybody!" A lot of minds flashed to a lot of things, but right then and there I could visualize my Christian mother down on her knees on a cold linoleum floor with a pair of homemade flannel pajamas on, praying for her baby boy Jerry. I knew she was doing this because so many times during my school days I'd get off the bus over on the main highway and walk through the woods to the house, ease in that old country home, and, being real quiet and careful not to wake up my mother, I'd see a shadow in her room—and as I peeped through the door, there she'd be praying for her children. And the prayers of Christian mothers follow their children.

The mother in the home is a stabilizer. She is the salt, she leavens the loaf, she makes sure that if there is a lack of communication or misunderstanding about to happen she repeats what was said so one person can understand the motive of the other one. She's also a mind-reader. A godly woman who lives in a home with her family knows more about the family than anyone else. It's remarkable how she can know what you're thinking.

A Christian home has rules. Yes, it even has laws. If you break a rule, we just talk to you. If you break one of the laws, you're in trouble. One of the laws we have is that on Sunday morning no one is ever allowed to ask the question: Are we going to church and Sunday school today? That is already answered and settled. It is not optional on the Lord's Day to get up and go to the House of the Lord. So many parents make the mistake of letting the children start discussing, "Should we go today?" Anytime you allow this discussion to come up, you will usually talk yourself out of going. But if you make it a law, it's automatic. Folks don't get up and say, "I wonder if I'm going to the office this morning." If it's a workday, go to work. If it's Sunday, go to church. My children, praise God, look forward to going to church more than any other thing they do. Now my young one, Katy, loves to go to the King of the Road Motel and go backstage at the Grand Ole Opry and visit with Dolly Parton. But she'd just as soon go to church and hear Bible stories.

It all boils down to the golden rule. Simply treat your children like you would want to be treated in their situation. Demand that your children respect and treat you like they would one day want their children to respect and treat them. As soon as the child can hear, make sure he or she understands who is the authority in the home and what discipline is. If you keep putting it off, the child will be so old that you will have lost him. Then he'll balk, and you'll have problems galore. If you've waited so long that your children are so big you can't control them, then do the best with what you can, but start doing it right now.

Years ago a co-worker got me off in a quiet place, shut the door, looked at me kind of funny, and said, "I don't like the way you treat Amy."

"What?! What in the world do you mean?"

"I know Amy doesn't run with any football, she can't tackle anybody, and she doesn't block anybody, and she doesn't swing the bat like your son Ray does. But I feel you're just a little more enthusiastic about the things Ray does than you are what Amy does."

I paused and swallowed hard three or four times, then I looked him right in the eye. "Fred, thank you. I appreciate you calling this to my attention." I felt guilty. I discussed this with my wife, we prayed about it, and from that day to this one I've done my dead-level best never to show partiality to one of my children. But suppose the word was out that I had reached the point of no approach and that I wouldn't have appreciated any advice. I pray to God I never will reach that point.

Finally, to have a Christian home, you must be yourself in the home. How tragic it is to be sweet and exhibit the paper smile and get on the David Frost show and let sugar drip from all around you, and go all over the country and be sweet to everybody, but come home and be a holy terror. You must be yourself.

A daddy is charged with the greatest responsibility of any living human being. He has to do some things sometimes that are distasteful. He has to do some things that take genuine backbone, such as saying no.

But if God be for him, who can be against him?

10

Prayers, Pet Peeves, and Pleasures

Hello, everybody. Today our special guest is Jerry Clower, the number one country comic in America, along with Madam Frances Judkins and three call girls.

STAN SIEGEL,
on "Mornings with Siegel,"
WLAC-TV, Nashville

JERRY CLOWER WITH a madam and three call girls? I didn't even know that they were going to be on there. I had walked on the show, wearing my loudest show clothes, because I was fixing to do the MCA Records Deejay Convention Show at the auditorium across the street from the TV studios.

So I was sitting there not knowing whether these women are going to come on while I'm on the air or not.

But this didn't bother me because I'm Jerry Clower twenty-four hours a day, and I react like Jerry Clower to whatever the situation is. I don't have to rehearse

and know way ahead of time what's going to happen.
I react based on my deep convictions, and I treat
other people like I want to be treated.

It turned out that I wasn't on at the same time as
the madam. Stan wouldn't risk it. I know what I
would have done. I would have said, "Look, this is
incomplete. Here's a madam and three girls—three
prostitutes—but where are your customers? For the
people who view this very fine TV show, this is incomplete. You girls have said it's a hundred dollars a
night. There ain't no folks with just average income
patronizing you unless they stole the money. I want
to see some of these folks that's making this kind of
money—some of these upstanding Nashville business-
men. I want your customer to sit here with you and
let his wife and children look into the face of who is
buying your services. Y'all go home and bring your
customers with you, and I'll interview you. This thing
of arresting you and not arresting your customers is
stupid. How could they have the audacity to say you're
breaking the law when there's no way you can break
the law unless you've got somebody tangoing with
you?"

"Hello, Jerry," Stan said. "Are you always this
happy? Or are you just putting on for the camera?"

"Stan, let me warn you, you don't want to get into
the line of discussion you're leading into. I know this
much about show business. You ought not to pursue
this."

"Aw, are you happy all the time? Or are you despondent like a lot of the rest of us?"

"I get up every morning and pray a very simple
prayer. 'Lord, I ain't going to work for you today. But
I want you to know I'm on your side. I'm willing for
you to use me today. I've turned all my hang-ups over
to the one what was hung up for my hang-ups.' I'm
on the road to heaven and happy about it. And, Stan,
I am Jerry Clower twenty-four hours a day and I am
this happy."

"You mean to tell me I cannot be as happy as you unless I'm a Christian?"

"I ain't told you that at all, Stan. I warned you that you didn't want to get into this, but you went on and pursued it anyhow. You asked me a simple question, and I gave you an honest answer. If you're despondent, you look into the TV camera, look at the red light, and you tell the folks why you're so unhappy. I just told them why I'm happy."

"Aw, well, I have the right not to be a Christian."

"Oh, Stan, hallelujah. I'm the most liberal religious-liberty fighting fellow you ever saw in your life. I fought a war to give you the right to go to hell if you want to."

"Wait a minute! Wait a minute, Jerry! No, I have a faith."

"Since you've brought all this up, let me ask you something. I went by the auditorium on the way over here and a policeman asked where I was going. I told him I was going over to be on the Stan Siegel show— what do folks in Nashville think about him? He said that half of them hate him and half of them love him —so consequently the half that hate him watch him, and the half that love him watch him . . . so everybody watches him. I asked what he thought about Stan and he said, 'I hate him.' I asked why, and he said, 'Because he's an atheist.' Stan, are you an atheist?'

"I have a faith."

We got into a discussion and he asked for telephone calls. The phone rang and this voice said, "Stan, you'll never understand how happy Jerry really is unless you do become a Christian."

"Forget that! I don't want to keep pursuing this line of questioning."

I said, "You're the one who started it. You brought it up, so you answer the woman's question."

"I'm not going to answer it. I do have a faith. Next question."

It was a teen-age girl. "Mr. Clower, it's very easy for you to be happy. It's very easy for you to enjoy life—

you have four hit records, you're the top country comedian in the nation, and you make a lot of money."

"Darling, you have missed the point altogether. I'm so glad you called and asked this question. I know a lot of folks richer than me that are miserable. They're not happy under any circumstances."

After I had finished the show, something happened that's a fine illustration of how God answers prayers. I believe with every fiber of my being that the Lord answers every prayer. He either says yes or no.

While leaving the studio for the auditorium to kick off the MCA show which was going to start soon, two men who looked like business executives approached me.

"Mr. Clower, can we chat with you just a minute?"

"Yessir."

"I'm pastor of an Assembly of God church here in Nashville, and this is my friend who is the guest evangelist at our church this week. Monday we came down here and talked to Stan Siegel and asked to be on this show, and he said that we couldn't—that he'd had enough talk about churches and religion of late. So we went back home and we all prayed in our church that the Lord would be glorified on the Stan Siegel show somehow this week. We got up this morning and dressed to get ready to start our day of revival effort and visitation. We turned on the television, and there is the most unlikely fellow that we would have ever thought God would have used to answer our prayer. But that was one of the most beautiful Christian testimonies we ever heard. Not only did we have a prayer of praise and thanksgiving, we said, 'Lord, thank you for answering our prayer'—but we wanted to drive down here and tell you how God has used you this morning."

So now it's no mystery why Stan just kept insisting and asking me questions in such a manner that the only way I could answer it was to give my Christian testimony. God's folks prayed, and the Lord apparently wanted the prayer answered.

Why do I feel more at ease with Frances Judkins and her girls than I do with Jerry Clower? Because Jerry is very judgmental, and the girls aren't.

STAN SIEGEL

There's nothing I believe in as a Christian any more than prayer. It's something I can do as an individual and go direct to the Lord. I don't have to go through any exchange anywhere or get permission from anybody. And the Lord never makes a mistake in whatever he wants to say to me. That suits me fine.

Clower may be one of the few current-day Christians whose prayers the Lords looks forward to, if they are anything at all like the rest of his conversation, and if such odd elements as punting statistics keep turning up in them.

Sports Illustrated

At the end of a prayer meeting at my church, I was asked if it's harder for me to live a Christian life now than it used to be. Well, there's more temptation now. And there's no test of a Christian like prosperity. The greatest test of a man's Christian faith is to be prosperous.

They also asked if I meet many good Christian people in show business. I meet about the same percentage as I did when I was in the fertilizer business. One lady spoke up and claimed, "It's very obvious that show business people marry more and do more bad things than the average folks." I asked her to pause and look around at the little town where she lived and at some of the things that were happening to some prominent people there. Had those people been show business personalities, the news would have gotten in all the papers. Since they weren't in the public eye as much as show business folks, it wasn't publicized as much.

Some of my friends are a little bit aggravated with

me because I haven't received the gift of speaking in tongues. I know of some excellent churches which were split right down the middle because some of the folks started speaking in tongues and some of the other folks didn't get this gift. I won't ever underestimate the power of the Holy Spirit. I believe that God can give anybody any gift he wants them to have, but he has never given me the gift of speaking in tongues and I don't aim to do it unless he specifically gives me that gift. Some individuals were called on by some of these folks who speak in tongues and told to throw their crutches down or put their medicine down because God had given them the gift of speaking in tongues and he would heal them. Some of them ended up in the insane asylum because the medicine was taken from them. I wouldn't do any criticizing or point a finger at anybody, but I'll tell you one thing—anytime something happens to hurt the cause of Christ, it's no kind of gift from God. You write that down. I've seen happy Christian couples in the church, then one of them would get this gift of speaking in tongues and it'd end up in unhappiness . . . at home, and in the church. God is not the father of any kind of unhappiness.

My pet peeve is taking something simple and making it complicated. Folks work at this all the time.

In a shopping center I wanted a cup of coffee. Well, they don't call coffee shops "coffee shops" any more. They name them something else. I saw a big sign and it said Boutique. I figured that was a coffee shop and opened the door. What they were doing was hemming a woman's dress. They were selling women's dresses.

"Where's the coffee?"

"It's on down the shopping mall."

I saw a sign that said Coiffure. So I figured that was the coffee. Uh huh, I've found me some coffee. I opened the door and they were teasing a woman's hair. So I never did get any coffee.

Coffee shops ought to be called coffee shops, cafes ought to be called cafes, and hamburger joints ought to be called hamburger joints. Take the plain preparing of food. Some restaurants have to hire extra help and really work at it to mess it up as bad as they do. If they'd be simple, the food would taste a lot better.

I'm going to take a trip with an individual, and we plan to leave at nine o'clock. Well, he'll call me fifteen times: "Are we still going to leave at nine?" Why do you want to discuss it? Lord have mercy, some folks aren't happy unless they're making a simple thing complicated.

It's the trend, it's fashionable, now to have one of those duodenal ulcers. If you ain't got a duodenal ulcer, you ain't in it. A dear friend of mine had one and stayed in the hospital two weeks, and liked to have died. He spent thousands of dollars and finally got home—and a black friend told him to take a little baking powder for it. He did. And he has never felt so good in his life. And the black friend didn't charge him a dime. It was getting fashionable to have a big duodenal ulcer, but he found out it was simple to care for it—so it really disappointed him.

Another peeve is for folks to say they're sick when they aren't. I feel so strongly about this that I'm not patient with folks who are sick. I don't have the compassion I ought to have for sick folks. Never have had it. Because in my entire life, I've never been sick. I had the diverticulitis one time. My stomach hurt a little bit and I went to the hospital for some check-ups. On occasions I might have had some of those things that put other folks in the bed. It's kind of like the times. You go talking about how sorry the times are, and it isn't long before you can talk yourself into a depression. Some people talk themselves into being depressed and sick. If you aren't sick, don't act like you are sick. I never took a sleeping pill in my life—I have no trouble sleeping. If you get tired enough, you sleep. I hate to sleep. I'd stay up all the time if I could. If I could find somebody to talk to, I'd stay up all night.

I require just a little bit of sleep. I can go to bed and get four hours and be ready to go. Or eight hours.

Or six hours. I can still be tired, but the Lord's been good to me—I can be dragging and get ready to do a show, put on those show clothes, run out on stage, and that light hits me, the adrenalin starts flowing, and I'm not tired at all. I jump and holler and kick and whoop. But the minute I walk off the stage, I'm tired again. This might not be a good sign. I might be causing adrenalin to flow when I ought to be resting.

I don't have any worldly ambitions, but I promised if I ever got me enough money, I was going to buy me one of those big long cars. And I bought me one recently—you have to go to the airport to turn it around. I was putting that premium gas in it, and the fellow at the service station said, "This thing will burn regular gas and burn it better than it will premium."

"You could hear it knocking all the way to Nashville, Tennessee, if you put some of that cheap gas in it."

"Look, have you read the operator's manual?"

"You know, sir, that's a good lesson for me. General Motors made this car. They ought to know more about it than anybody else because they made it. The folks that made it wrote the book telling me how to operate it. Looks like they know more about it than I do." I looked in the book, and it said burn regular. Folks, it burns regular better than it does premium. I got to thinking: Jerry, God made you, and if he made you he ought to know more about you than anybody else. He, too, has written an operator's manual. It's called the Bible. So you want to know how to live? Look in there! If you don't understand it, God said pray—and he'd let you understand it.

Let's keep it simple. Hell's hot, heaven's wonderful, and those who know Jesus Christ as their own personal savior are going to miss hell and hit heaven. Period! The Bible says there's no other way to get to heaven other than through the Lord Jesus Christ who died on the cross for our sins. If it wasn't necessary for him to die to save me, then God murdered him for nothing.

Speaking of simplicity, I had also said that if I ever

got enough money I was going to buy one of those big Rolex watches. I went to the store and said, "Lay them out. My record's done sold a million dollars' worth. I want to look at those pretty gold Rolex watches." They laid them out, but none of them had numbers on them. "Don't you have watches with numbers on them?"

"Sir, our watches have Roman numerals."

"I didn't grow up in Rome. I growed up at Rt. 4, Liberty, Mississippi, finished East Fork Consolidated High School, and we didn't teach them Roman numerals because we didn't have any Romans going to school there. I don't believe in them none, and I get mad every time I see a Roman numeral."

"Well, sir, I'm sorry."

"You can be sorry, but how about making me one of these big fancy watches and put a dollar Sears and Roebuck face on it." And they did. I wear the only Rolex watch ever specially made with numbers on it. It was worth fifteen hundred dollars when I bought it; it's worth three thousand dollars now. Because of the gold price, they doubled in value in one year. A three-thousand-dollar watch with a dollar Sears and Roebuck face on it.

The greatest form of paganism we portray today is folks who claim to be Christians at weddings and funerals. No doubt about it. Especially at weddings. It beats all I ever saw.

I was in the wedding of two Christian folks, and during rehearsal I asked, "Where's the young lady what's going to get married?"

"She's sitting out in the audience."

"Why ain't she rehearsing?"

"It's bad luck."

"Whaaaat?"

"It's bad luck. Are you crazy? Have you lost your mind? Don't nobody with no sense rehearse their own wedding because it's bad luck."

"Well, why don't you send to Africa and get you one of them voodoo oongawa witch doctors with a bone in his nose, and let him dangle a dying chicken and sling blood all over everybody, and burn some incense."

"Aw, Mr. Clower! Why do you want to be that way?"

"Because y'all are paganistic. It would make just as much sense to let a witch doctor run up and down the aisle at a so-called Christian wedding as it would to say she can't rehearse her wedding because it's bad luck." It's so pitiful, so pagan.

When my daughter, bless her heart, got married, we didn't even play "Here Comes the Bride." We played a hymn. I was so proud—it thrilled me to death. We're Christian folk so we played a hymn when they walked in the church. One lady at my church tells me every time she sees me, "I don't feel like Amy is married. I never did hear 'Here Comes the Bride.' "

At my daughter's wedding rehearsal they said, "Who gives this bride away?"

"Jerry and Homerline Clower," I said.

A woman grabbed her chest and fell backwards and screamed—and you could have heard her all the way to Texas: "Ohhh, Mr. Clower! Ohhh, Lord!"

"Woman, what's wrong with you?"

"That's not the way you say it. Let me tell you how Amy Vanderbilt says you're supposed to do it."

"Did Amy Vanderbilt ever have a hit record about a coon hunt?"

"What?"

"Amy Vanderbilt should have checked with me about having a wedding. I ain't going to check with her. This is me and my children. She didn't put a dime in this. We're in a church, it's a Christian church, and a Christian man is going to marry my child. And we'll do what we please." The world is in a mess until folks start doing that. People read books and call up specialists—"We want to do this right; how are you supposed to do it?" You are supposed to do it within the confines of your Christian conviction. As long as it's Christian, do it! Confound all that pagan stuff!

One of the things that bothers me most is getting so many requests to speak as a Christian entertainer. I get about 150 invitations a month. When I first started in show business, I decided to handle all of my Christian requests or church-related requests myself. It got so large that all I'd do when I was at home was to try to handle it. There was no way I could make a commitment to come at a certain time and speak in a church because, as I was doing it, Tandy Rice might be booking me at that very same minute somewhere else to work for some money. I prayed about it, talked to some of my friends about it, and decided to let Top Billing Agency—Tandy Rice—handle it all. When he gets a request from a church-related or Christian group or a preacher, he simply explains, "Jerry works two ways. He works for money and he works for nothing. What way are you talking about?"

If they say, "We're talking about him giving his Christian testimony and coming when he can for nothing," he will explain: "Great. He tithes his time just like he does his money. We'll try to work it in the very first chance we get."

Sometimes they'll say, "Wait a minute—we want him now. We may sell tickets and rent an auditorium. What would it take to get him?" Then Tandy will tell them. On occasion I've gotten letters from some of the preachers and they were ugly to me . . . talked bad. It bothered me so bad. I want the world to know that it doesn't cost anything for me to give my Christian testimony. That ain't the way it works.

From the fourth Sunday in July when I was thirteen, in 1939, every decision I made was based on the fact that I am a new creature in Christ—I'm a Christian. I don't make decisions now like I once did. From that day to this one, my foot has slipped, I have messed up, I have had a lot of problems I didn't know the solution to, but I knew I had been saved by an almighty God that had the solution. And I was on his side. That's the way I have lived.

After having gone through the service, I rededicated

my life to Christ, started praying that prayer every morning—and have been doing it ever since. In the navy as a seventeen-year-old kid going overseas, I didn't know anything. I was long-headed—it was a wonder I didn't get killed. A kamikaze would dive into the ship I was on, and it didn't scare me too bad. I didn't have enough sense to know what danger was.

There was one thing I never could get adjusted to. We'd shoot down a Japanese airplane, and the old hands on the ship would cheer. They'd actually yell like cheerleaders at the death of the man. I never did get any satisfaction out of cheering even though he was an enemy and we had killed him.

I never could do that even though he was trying to kill me. If I killed him, it was sad.

11

Yazoo City Yarns

Through the years, the American Society of Composers, Authors and Publishers has had many illustrious members who were masterful artists with words, but no one has captured the soul and humor of a region as powerfully and capably as Jerry Clower. He hails from an oral tradition that has given us other story tellers like Mark Twain and Will Rogers, authors like William Faulkner and James Dickey, and songwriters like Johnny Mercer and Hank Williams. In giving voice to the South, Jerry has a message for the entire nation . . . and the world. A message of Christianity, comedy, and compassion.

ED SHEA
Southern Director, ASCAP

IT TAKES ONE secretary and near about one full day a week to send back material that I'm mailed. Stuff that folks send me that they want me to write or record. I don't mind receiving this stuff if folks wouldn't lie to me. Ninety percent of it I've heard all my life, and people say, "This is original with me—I wrote it." Sometimes at a show somebody will get hold of me and they just know they've written a hit, and won't I record it? I try to have compassion and treat these folks like I'd want them to treat me.

It galled me to have to unlist my phone number. I enjoy talking to people. But you can't do that all the time—you've got to sleep sometime. It's a great compliment that some very fine writers and superstar artists have sent me material to look over, and I can see down the road where I will record some of it. I don't think I'll ever run out of material. People ask who writes for me. Nobody writes for me up to now. As I think of things or see things that reminds me of a story I could use on a record, I make a note, put it in my pocket, and, later, file it in a tray on my desk. The week I make the album I get out all these notes, go over them, pick out my favorites and do the album. As long as I travel around and have experiences, I'll get new stories. Take my woman's lib story that has done so well on the "Country Ham" album. I got that from an encounter with a woman libber on the Mike Douglas show.

I had an encounter with the She-Coon of all the Women Libbers in the world. I'm not knocking women liberators—I've been one all my life, and I've been willing for a lady to make wages like a man if she did a man's job. I'm minding my own business waiting to be called to come out on the big talk show before millions of people, and the She-Coon comes walking in to the room. I know she's a female as to how her dungarees are fitting her. I got up and said, "Lady, take my chair."

"You sit down!"

"Ma'am?"

"You sit down!"

"My ancestors would come up out of the grave

and get me if I did. I have been taught all my life to stand up and give a lady a chair."

"You sit down!"

"I ain't gonna do it!"

So she sat down in the middle of the floor to embarrass me. Left me standing by the vacant chair.

"Lady, I wouldn't embarrass you for nothing in the world. I am a man what don't believe in embarrassing lady folks, and I want to do what's right. Tell me, what all women are you liberating?"

"Every female in America. Some phase of her life I intend to liberate."

"Let me tell you about me and mama. Wooo! Me and mama has been married twenty-six years. She was my childhood sweetheart. I ain't never had another date. Mama sleeps every morning until she gets ready to get up. Now she might have to get up at eight o'clock and unlock the door to let the lady in what I got hired to wait on mama. Yeah. And when mama does get up, she can fix her own breakfast or have it brought to her. It'll be mama's option, whichever way she wants it. And when mama watches them soap operas, she can watch it in three different rooms in the house—laying down, leaning, or propped up . . . whichever way she wants to do it. And when mama gets ready to go to the supermarket or get her hair fixed, she goes in a brand new *gold* Lincoln Continental. Mizz Woman Libber, mama don't want you messing with the deal she's got."

That's how I get my stories. These things happen to me and I tell them.

I was there when Jerry and Gloria Steinem got into it—and a very strange thing happened. Pearl Bailey was there, too, and she and Jerry had really hit it off great. When Gloria attacked Jerry, Pearl Bailey rushed to his defense and said, "Ma'am, it's wonderful to be able to find a real gentleman nowadays." It was really something! Here was this great black lady defending this white man from the South.

JOHN BROWN
MCA Records

The way I got another story . . . I was flying into Chattanooga, and the lady TV personality met me at the airport. She had a microphone in her hand and a guy with her who held a big TV camera on his shoulder. I stepped off the big Delta jet, and she said, "Welcome to Chattanooga."

"Thank you, ma'am."

"How does it feel to go from a fertilizer salesman to the nation's top country comedian?"

"Feels gooooood!"

"I read in your press kit sent out by your agency that you are a Christian man—you have a home where love is, you have four children, and I want to know what your reaction is to this new fad of streaking."

"New fad? Lady, how come you city folks are calling that new?"

"Oh? What did you call it when you were growing up?"

"Running naked. Have you ever played Gator at the swimming hole?"

"Pardon?"

"Gator at the swimming hole. Us boys used to go down there, and we'd hang our overalls on a willow bush on the back of the swimming hole, and we'd get off in the water buck naked. We would select a gator— we'd pick somebody to catch us in the water, and we'd call him the gator just like city folks play tag—they say, 'You are It.' If you couldn't outswim the gator, you had to take to the woods to see if you could out-run him. If you were seen from a public road running naked, you were in trouble. And if you came within sight of a public road, you doubled back because if somebody had sent word to your papa that you were running naked, you would have *got* streaked. In my personal opinion that's what ought to happen to these modern-day streakers. My papa needs to put that dried brush broom right up under the soft part of their sitting down place—and they'd cover themselves up and wouldn't be running naked through any public place."

Another way I get some of my material is by simply observing other artists. One of the dearest people in all of show business is Loretta Lynn. While in Nashville to do the "Hee Haw" show, I was on the set with Stringbean—bless his heart, I miss him so much. The cue was from Stringbean, and he said, "Have you met any nice people since you've been in show business?"

"Yeah. Thank God for Loretta Lynn. I have at long last met somebody what's as country as I am. And I growed up country. You know I can unwind the well windlass where the bucket will go down in the well and you can fill up the bucket and draw up a bucket of water and won't even disturb the well. I got that country touch. I can keep a setting hen from quitting the nest just by clucking to her. I can put a can of Hi-Life in a big drum of shell peas and the Hi-Life will seep out and kill every weevil in them peas, but it won't kill you if you eat the peas. I'm country enough to know how to kill them weevils in them peas. I can prepare chitlings—fresh, creek-slung, or stump-whupped. I am that country. But up beside Loretta Lynn, I am a city slicker."

Both Loretta and I love those shoot'em-up Western movies. We like to see them bust those caps. You know Loretta went to see *Midnight Cowboy* because she thought it was a shoot'em-up Western—and her band members let her go on. Bless her heart, when some of those things started happening in that movie, Loretta said, "What in the world is this here?"

The coon-hunt story is the mainmost story of them all. Wherever I go and do a show, people demand that I tell it.

John Eubanks was a great American—he was a professional tree climber. He didn't believe in shooting no coon out of no tree—it was against his upbringing. He taught us from birth—from the day we were born—to the age we could keep listening to him, "Give every thing a sportin' chance. Whatever you do, give it a sportin' chance." He would have been a great conservationist today if he'd be here. John said, "Take a cross-cut saw coon hunting with you. When you tree a coon, hold the dogs and cut the tree down, or either climb the tree and make the coon jump in amongst the dogs. Give him a sportin' chance."

A lot of times, we'd climb a tree and make a coon jump in amongst twenty dogs, but at least he had the option of whipping all them dogs and walking off if he wanted to. This was strictly left up to the coon.

We hollered, and the dogs started hunting. We listened, and directly old John Eubanks hollered, "Speak to him!"

About that time they treed him. We rushed down into the swamps, and there the dogs were treed up the biggest Sweetgum tree in all of Amite River Swamps. It was huge—you couldn't reach around this tree. There wasn't a limb on it for a while. Way up there. Huge tree.

I looked around at John, and I said, "John, I don't believe you can climb that tree." And it hurt John's feelings. He pooched his lips out. He got fighting mad. He said, "There ain't a tree in all of these swamps that I can't climb."

He got his brogan shoes off and eased up to that Sweetgum tree, and he hung his toenails in that bark and he got his fingernails in there, and he kept easing up the tree, working his way toward that bottom limb, and he finally got to it and he started on up into this big tree.

"Knock him out, John! It won't be long."

John worked his way on up to the top of the tree: "Wooooo, what a big one!" He reached around in his overalls and got that sharp stick and he drawed back and he punched the coon. But it wasn't a coon. It was a lynx. We call them souped-up wildcats in Amite County. And that thing had great big tusks coming out of its mouth. And great big claws on the end of its feet. And, people, that thing attacked John up in top of that tree.

WAAAAOOOOOHH! You could hear John squawling.

"What's the matter with John?"

"I don't have no idea."

"What in the world's happening to John?"

"Knock him out, John."

WAAAOOOOHH! "This thing's killing me!"

The whole top of the tree was shaking. The dogs got to biting the bark of the tree and fighting one another underneath the tree, and I was kicking them back.

"What's the matter with John?"

"Knock him out, John."

WAAAAAOOOOOOOO!! "This thing's killing me!" And John knew Mr. Barron toted a pistol in his belt to shoot snakes with it. And he kept hollering, "Wooo, shoot this thing. Have mercy, this thing's killing me. Shoot this thang!'"

And Mr. Barron said, "Johnnnn! I can't shoot up in there. I might hit *you*."

John said, "Well, just shoot up in here amongst us. One of us has got to have some relief."

One of the great problems we have in America today is that people act and live a life based on who's seeing them. I've seen some politicians talking and they found out somebody in the crowd was a reporter, and they got to fidgeting and tried to change everything they said. And this is a sin before God. I've got a story that's a good example of this.

Me and Sonny was up in the corn crib killing them rats as we got to them. Sonny caught a big one in the throat—it was the most hugest rat I'd ever seen in my life. It was such a fine rat that my brother Sonny wanted to show it to mama. Now Sonny didn't know that Rev. Brock the Baptist preacher was in the house visiting with mama. She was sitting in one corner—the preacher was in the other. Sonny ain't seen the preacher yet. He rushed into the living room and said, "Looka here at what a rat. I done whupped him over the head with an ear of corn. I done jobbed him with a hay fork. I done stripped all the hide off of his tail. I done whipped him up and down on the floor. I done stomped him three or four times, and—" And then Sonny saw the preacher. He hugged that rat up to his chest and commenced to fondling it and stroking it and crying and saying, ". . . and then the Lord called the poor thing home."

Now my mama wanted the rat dead. He was eating up our corn, he was wetting in our shucks when we had to feed them to our cows—we shucked and shelled corn to go to the mill, and that nasty thing had messed it up. She wanted him dead, and Sonny knew she wanted him dead, and he was so proud to show her the big dead rat, he didn't know what to do. And he had beat him and stomped him, but when he saw the preacher he wanted to change his tune.

People ought to be who they are. I don't say anything any day that I wouldn't want my pastor to hear. I don't tell you any stories where you have to look around and say, "Are there any women here?" My albums have proved that. I'm human enough that I appreciate what my albums have done because I was told before I made the one which went to the top ten in the nation that unless I put a little risqué vulgar stuff on it, I'd never be known nationally. People, I've got

news for you. There ain't none of them who gave me
that advice who ever had one in the top ten. This ought
to tell folks something. This is one reason I'm booked
so much; the word's out that I'm a family entertainer.

When Jerry tells you a story, you know you've
been told a story. If it's just you and he, he has
got you by the arm and is cuffin' you on the back
and carryin' on something furious. If he's performing, he cackles, snorts, whoops, stomps, shouts,
weeps, gulps, mugs, agonizes, sweats. He can imitate a diesel truck, a motorcycle, a Brahma bull,
a chain saw. . . . Most of all, he can imitate a
classic prissy. Like when he tells of a record-
company fellow coming to Yazoo City to talk
about record contracts and "he come skippin' off
that airplane, big funny-lookin' hairdo all pushed
up, silly-lookin' pants. Then he told me how much
cash money he had in that brief case, and suddenly
my attitude got a lot more tolerant about his
hairdo."

The National Observer

People ask me all the time if Marcel Ledbetter ever
got in any trouble besides the time he took the chain
saw and ran them out of the beer joint. And the
answer is—one other time.

What he did . . . he and his younger brother Claude
sneaked into the East Fork Baptist Church and poured
all the grape juice out of the communion bottles and
replaced it with green persimmon wine. And the next
Lord's Day, they served the Lord's Supper. Everybody
in the whole church house partook. And when the
preacher got done partaking, he got up and tried to
talk, but his lips were pooched out so he just puckered
up. He announced, speaking the best he could with his
lips pooched out, "As is our custom, we'll stand and
sing our closing hymn." And they all got up and
whistled the closing hymn.

He takes a situation and it becomes dramatic. I've heard him tell the same story twenty times— and you never get the feeling it's stereotyped. It comes out fresh every time with a little bit different interpretation and wordage.

He's a very competent entertainer now. It's a facet of his salesmanship. He's a good salesman, period. Entertainment is largely salesmanship— he's selling a brand of humor.

OWEN COOPER
Mississippi Chemical Corporation

Ninety-nine percent of everything I say is almost the truth. I do very little listening to, or reading, other story tellers because I feel like sometime when I'm recording that I might unconsciously get a line from them. I've never heard all of Wendy Bagwell's stuff. The only thing I've ever heard him do is what I've heard on the radio—and I wouldn't listen to all of it because it would remind me of things I could develop a story on. I love Wendy. He's one of the world's best story tellers, and he's a strong Christian.

Jeanne Pruett told me a story that I've got on record. Jimmy Gately told me one. One of these days I'm going to do an album—"Stories I Have Heard."

My grandfather used to tell stories about sawmill happenings. It was about some of my kinfolks. I had an uncle named Stan Hill, and Uncle Stan used to tell stories about World War I. I knew half of it wasn't so. He was exaggerating.

Someone asked my mother how long I had been a talker. She said she never remembered a time when I wasn't talking. I don't sit around thinking up a lot of stuff. It just comes out.

A few years ago I received an award for being the leading citizen in the community of Brook-haven—the Soap Box Award. I sent Jerry a copy of it and said, "Jerry, you had a great part in me receiving this Soap Box award." As full of humor as Jerry is, he called me and said, "Anybody who gets the Soap Box Award, it sounds like from what they say that you need a bath."

One time Jerry wanted a puppy. I had a half Basset Hound, half Beagle named Percy that I gave him. Percy later appeared in a TV commercial eating dog food out of Katy's hand. So I called Jerry and said, "I'm thinking I ought to get some of the proceeds from Percy." He wrote me back and told me, "I've turned it over to the attorney general for a ruling on this, and he says you're entitled to nothing. But since I've talked to you on the phone, Percy has bit a man, and there's a $200,000 lawsuit pending. What percent of Percy do you want?"

ALCUS SMITH
Brookhaven, Mississippi

One night I was walking across the breakfast room in my shorts going to the refrigerator to get a glass of skim milk. The phone rang.

"Talk to me!"

"Hello, Jerry, it's Charlie Douglas, WWL, New Orleans."

"Hey, Charlie, how're you doing?"

"We're calling several of the artists who have hit records—and we're asking them what does Christmas mean. Jerry, we've got less than four minutes, the tape's running, and we're going to be playing this on the air. What does Christmas mean to you?"

"Christmas means to me: Bob Hope going to Vietnam, the smell of a mellow apple, passing cars on the highway and they've got Christmas packages piled up in the back of them and you know they're going visiting, kissing kinfolks—some of them you enjoy kissing and some of them you don't, heartburn, eating too much, goodies all around the house, telephone ringing and 'Hello, daddy—I found a beautiful present for mother—can I buy it and charge it to you?' kids screaming—'Daddy, they won't let me put the icicles on the tree and they're keeping me from decorating the tree and make them let me put the icicles up there on the top limb! . . .' Oh, Christmas is beautiful. A great time around the Clower household. Christmas. But, Charlie, the other day my little girl came in from a shopping center and she said she saw another little girl sitting in Santa Claus's lap and the girl told Santa, 'There ain't a dime in our house. We ain't got a penny. And my mother said we wasn't going to get nothing for Christmas.'

"I said, 'Darling, what was her name? Let's go find her.' Me and my little Sue went and found her. And we bought her a Christmas tree. We decorated it. We bought her a baby doll. We left some money at the corner grocery store. They could come there all during the Christmas season to get some groceries on the money we left for them.

"What's Christmas? It's the expression on that little girl's face when she saw somebody loved her enough to make sure that she, too, was going to have a Christmas. Why did my family react to this situation like we did? It's because we don't have a pagan Christmas. We know the Christ child—the one who was born at Bethlehem. And we have followed him all the way through to Calvary, and we've put our faith and trust in this Christ child, and we're Christians. We worship him in spirit and in truth—and we reacted at Christmastime like Christian folks ought to react all of the time. Woooo, man, ain't it wonderful to be here at Christmastime! Praise God, ain't it great to be an American at Christmastime!"

After I had finished, there was a long pause on the phone. I finally said, "Charlie?"

Charlie was crying.

12

Ain't Life Great!

IT WAS A red hot Saturday afternoon in the heart of Amite County, and the old country store was alive. The people who could not go to McComb on Saturday afternoon would go to the store and buy things for the weekend or sit around and talk.

The hottest selling items in this store were stage planks, moon pies, cold Cokes, strawberry, and orange —if the ice truck from McComb happened to run that day. You could buy oil sausage from a big can in the back of the store. You'd take two small paper bags, put one down in the other, then take a long fork and stick these sausages, and you could get them one, two, or three at a time. There were loose crackers you could buy, and you could make a meal from this. Another hot seller was old rat cheese, also called hoop cheese. You could get a six-cent sack of Old North State smoking tobacco, and the most economical buy on cigarette papers was a nickel book of ABC papers. Some folks bought Country Gentleman smoking tobacco, and Prince Albert was a good seller, too.

This hot July afternoon, people were sitting around, some drinking RC Colas, some talking about the crops, when all of a sudden walking down the road hand in hand were two fellows, Bully and Simmie. It was obvious from their appearance that they had been drinking some of that old popskull whiskey that was made somewhere in Amite County.

They walked into the store and purchased a can of mustard sardines. Now this is a big, flat, oblong-shaped can, and these sardines are packed in a mustard sauce. Bully and Simmie carried the sardines outside and sat down on two RC Cola cases. They got their pocket knives out and, after whittling the top of the can open and bending back the jagged edge, Bully put the can of sardines down into the palm of his hand, and they started eating this delicacy right out of the can with their fingers.

Juice was dripping off their elbows, they got some of the sardines in their hair and eyebrows, the flies swarmed around them, but they kept eating the sardines, talking loud and bragging about what all they had going for them.

While this feast of the sardines was going on, up walked another fellow by the name of Louis. He was cross-eyed. Louis was staring right at them, but his head was turned looking across the road. Now friends, if you had seen this sight, you wouldn't have wanted anything to eat for at least a month. This was a bad-looking sight.

But Louis kept staring right at Bully and Simmie eating the sardines, digging into the can, and smacking their lips over the fine food they were eating. After Louis had stood there several minutes and heard Bully speak in a deep voice about how good they were, he walked into the store. "Mr. Charles," Louis asked the man who owned the store, "where are those sardines?"

"Louis, they are up there on the shelf."

And Louis said, "Well, get me a can of them because Bully has done flung a craving on me."

I heard a conversation recently where they decided that one way we can help the mess the world is in today is to go back to the good old days.

There are several things about the good old days I remember about my childhood that I'd like to go back to. But if you are talking about drawing that water, cutting that stove wood, chinching cracks when the cold wind blows, shucking and shelling corn and taking it to the mill, getting the hogs back in when they break out, milking the cows with the tail full of cockleburs hitting you beside the head, or if you are talking about dipping water out of the reservoir on the back of a stove on a cold Saturday night, sitting down on the edge of a No. 3 washtub and taking a bath . . . if that is the type of good old days you are talking about, then I want to go on record here and now and tell you, you can have them. But there are some things about the good old days I remember that I wish would come back.

When I was a kid, if you heard a bell ringing in the community and it wasn't dinnertime, then every person who heard the bell ran to help whoever was having a problem—because this was a distress signal. That's wonderful. If you gave a distress signal today, some individual people would come and check on you, but the entire community where you live, most of them could care less about your problem. In the past, if a home got burned out, when people came to see about it, a leader in the community would stand up and say, "Sam, you and your family bring a load of sweet potatoes. This couple over here, you bring corn, you bring several gallons of molasses, you bring a bucket of lard, you bring this, you bring that . . ." Assignments were made, and then came the announcement, "We're going to meet here tomorrow, and we're going to have a house building. We're going to build these people's house back."

That's a good part of the good old days—to be genuinely interested in your neighbor, and if you hear a
distress signal, go see about him and his problem. I
would like to see that come back into practice.

> Jerry brought back some memories that I
> cherish, but I was about to forget them.
>   ROY CLARK

The people back then were more sincere than they
are now. They simply were themselves. Being yourself
is an art. Some of my preacher friends lose their maximum effectiveness because they mock Billy Graham
when they preach. God didn't make but one Billy
Graham, and each person has to be himself or her-
self. I must admit that on occasion I've spoken at
some pretty fancy meetings and I've maybe tried to
impress the folks, but I fell flat on my face. In the
good old days, whatever you were, that's what you
were, and you were proud of it.

Back in those days we would get a bunch of friends
and neighbors together for a rat killing. They'd come
from all around, bringing their dogs and sticks. We
would get out in the corn crib and under the dairy
barn and the feed house and, man, we would forever-
more have some fun killing rats. We would even move
the whole crib of corn to get down to the rat nests so
we could kill those varmints. Our log crib sat way up
off the ground, and a bunch of my friends would stand
around and we'd get down to the corner where there
would be four or five bushels of corn left. We'd holler,
"Here they are, get ready!" Then we'd hit and knock
and good gracious alive, at the fun we'd have killing
those big rats and stacking them up in piles.

One day a bunch of those rats got away from us.
They ran through the circle and went under a big concrete slab at the milk shed. We drew water and poured
it down those holes; we even built a fire around the
washpot and heated some water and poured that scald-
ing water down the holes to kill the rats, but we

couldn't run them out. Somebody got the idea of trying to get an old A Model Ford cranked. We backed that thing up to the slab, got an old inner tube and made a pipe out of it, and put one end down in the rat hole under the concrete slab, and the other end around the exhaust pipe. We raced the motor and let the exhaust fumes go down into the holes. Friends, you've never had some real fun unless you have stood around a slab waiting for those carbon monoxided rats to come out from under there.

In the good old days we were poor, we didn't have much, but we did have those rat killings. And I expect if somebody had told us that we could petition the federal government to kill those rats for us, we wouldn't have done it because we were having too much fun killing them ourselves.

When I was a kid and someone let out an oath, often somebody would say, "Good gracious, that man cusses worse than Luther." I never thought about that much except I knew this fellow named Luther who was in the sawmill business. After I got older, I had the privilege of meeting Luther—and he wasn't the same individual he was when the people used to talk about him and his ways.

He told me why he had changed. He said that his wife was a Christian, and she was praying that he would come to know the Lord. But Luther refused to become a Christian. Luther had an old black friend whom he hunted and fished with, and who was a Christian. This black man, Uncle Ed Williams, used to camp out with Luther on the riverbank. They would set out hooks, and as they sat around the campfire, this old black man would look Luther in the eye and declare, "Sir, me and my wife are praying for you. We love you. We want to see you saved. You are too good a man not to give your heart to Jesus."

Luther would kind of make fun of Uncle Ed, and he would ask him, "How do you know you are saved?"

With a smile, Uncle Ed would tell him about the

book in the Bible where it says, "These things the Lord has done written unto me that if you believe in his name, you know you are saved."

So one night, knowing that Uncle Ed and his wife were praying for him, knowing that his own wife was praying for him, Luther got up out of his bed and went out in the sawmill. He got under conviction . . . the Holy Spirit convicted him of his sins. He knelt down, put his head against a piece of oak timber, and said, "Lord, have mercy on me, a sinner."

He confessed his sins and was gloriously saved. He went to the house, got back in bed, and slept until late in the morning—something he hadn't done in years. After he woke up, he told his wife what had happened to him, and she rejoiced. Then he told her, "I'm going down to the logging woods and see how all the hands are doing, and to tell my brother that I have become a Christian. Then I want to see Uncle Ed and tell him."

Luther walked across the plowed ground and saw old Uncle Ed plowing down in the field. Uncle Ed looked up, stopped his mule, and—before either of them said a word—he started walking around the mule, clapping his hands. "Mr. Luther's got it!" Uncle Ed yelled. "Mr. Luther's got it. Praise God, he's been saved!"

In all the things you do, you may be misunderstood, but it is hard to misunderstand love. If you convince folks you are interested in them because you love them, then you've just about got them—it's hard to fight love. I asked Luther what happened to Uncle Ed Williams.

"He's gone home to be with the Lord. You know, I run a country store—and after I was saved, I told Uncle Ed, 'You bring your eggs to my store, and I don't care what the price of eggs are, I'll give you a dollar a dozen. You can make a living by bringing eggs to my country store.' If they were a dime a dozen, I paid him a dollar. If they were thirty-five cents, I paid him a dollar. And I looked after him until the day God called him home. You know, he loved me . . . and he told me one day God would save me."

Luther became a Gideon—this is an association of Christian business and professional men who have banded themselves together to win men and women, boys and girls to the Lord Jesus Christ. I have been a Gideon for a long, long time.

The Baton Rouge Gideon Camp sponsored a Gideon Day at Angola Penitentiary. Gideons came from all over, bringing Bibles they bought themselves, going into the cells to tell the prisoners about the love of God, and giving them a New Testament. Luther walked into a cell and immediately a prisoner named Charlie Frazier started ridiculing and cursing him. In solitary confinement for twelve years, Charlie Frazier was a notorious criminal. He didn't want to talk to anybody, and he told Luther to get out. "You people come down here, you aren't confined, and it's easy for you to talk like you do."

Luther put his hand on Frazier's shoulder, looked him right in the eye, and a tear came down Luther's cheek. "Fellow, I just want to tell you that I love you."

Frazier ordered Luther out of the cell again. As Luther left, he laid a Testament on the bunk. "That's the Word of God. I hope you read it."

"You take your religion and live by it."

A few days later, Luther received a phone call. "Sir, I'm the chaplain at Angola Penitentiary. I"m calling to inform you that Charlie Frazier has been converted to Jesus Christ."

Frazier became superintendent of the Sunday school at Angola Penitentiary—a position he held until he was stricken with cancer. He was transferred to a hospital in New Orleans where he was shackled to the bed. Luther intervened and got a message to the governor of Louisiana. The governor checked with the attorney general, and they released this man from his shackles after Luther promised the authorities he would take full responsibility for Frazier's actions. There were no handcuffs shackling Charlie Frazier to the bed when he died. He had left his earthly possessions to Luther

—and he had told Luther that he loved him before he died.

The Louisiana attorney general was quoted as saying in the New Orleans paper, "We don't know what changed Frazier. He was a notorious criminal. He killed two guards in an attempt to escape from our penitentiary, but in the last few years he has been a new man. I don't know what came over him, but whatever it was changed his life."

Certainly, Christian people know what changed his life.

When I was a little boy, one of the prized possessions in the community was a coon dog named Little Red. He was the runt of the litter and was fed with a bottle until he grew up to be an outstanding coon dog.

One night we were hunting down in the swamps, and Little Red got cut on a cross-cut saw. I picked him up and started crying as I held his back leg where the saw had slashed him badly. I walked toward the main road so we could get the old Ford cranked and take Little Red into McComb to Dr. Williams, the veterinarian. We rushed to McComb and stopped at Gillis's Drug Store, but it was closed. When we got out of the car, my overalls were stiff from the dog bleeding on me. I had held his back leg, and every time his heart beat, the blood would gush out. I held the leg with my hand as hard as I could until the blood coagulated around my fingers.

All of the store lights were out except in the back where Mr. Gillis, the owner, was counting up the day's receipts. We knocked on the door, and Mr. Gillis came to it, eased it open a little, and asked, "What do you boys want?"

There we stood with our overalls on, dog blood all over me . . . scared to death. "Sir, don't the veterinarian rent an office from you?'"

"Yes, its upstairs. But he's out of town and won't be back until morning. What's the matter?"

"My coon dog is bleeding to death, and we need some help."

"I'm sorry, Dr. Williams won't be back until tomorrow. But bring your coon dog into the store, put him down there on the floor, turn the lights on, and let me see if I can help you."

The floor was spotless; you could smell the disinfectant where somebody had just mopped it clean. When I put the dog down, blood spread all over the floor. Mr. Gillis examined the leg. "Man, he's cut bad."

He went to the telephone, called his family physician, and told him the veterinarian was out of town but we needed to know how to put a pressure bandage on the dog's cut leg so the bleeding would stop. The medical doctor told him how to do it—and Mr. Gillis did it, and then gave the dog some drugs from his store.

"Son, you go on home. I'll put the dog on my back porch, and we'll see that Dr. Williams sees this dog just as soon as he gets to town in the morning."

Little Red lived to hunt again. Mr. Gillis could have run me off that sidewalk. He could have said, "You country boys get back out there with those other rednecks—and get that filthy bleeding dog out of here."

Yes, he could have run us off, and I probably would have hated him the rest of my life. But that's not the case. He set the proper example before two young boys and made a lasting impression. Ever since that night I have been looking for a boy with a hurt dog so I could give him some assistance. Because I know how thrilled he would be if some adult took the right attitude toward his problem.

I thank God for men like Norman B. Gillis, Sr., because he showed a young boy how adults are supposed to treat youngsters with problems.

So many adults don't have time for young people. Here is an example of how adults should be willing to counsel with youths. Our phone rang one Sunday, and it was my son, Ray. "Mama, where is my daddy?"

"He's coming in off a tour. He'll be at the house

when the girls and I get in from the church at twelve o'clock."

"If I leave Mississippi State now, I can get there by 12:30. I've got to talk to him."

Ray got there at 12:30 and didn't even say, "What's for dinner?" He got me by the elbow, we started down the hall, went to the bedroom, and he shut the door. He sat down on the bed and I sat on the chair. We were knee to knee. This is nothing new. When he was growing up, he would come in from a date, wake me up, sit on the edge of the bed, and talk to me for an hour.

"Daddy, you know I've been trying to decide what I'm going to do with my life. I got into business and I didn't like it. I got into economics and agriculture because, very frankly, that's what you majored in and I knew you could get some company you do commercials for to give me a job. But I wasn't sure. And I felt like maybe I wanted to coach. I got me an appointment with Coach Bob Tyler over at Mississippi State. He's a professional. So my appointment was yesterday at 9:30. I went in and said, 'Coach Tyler, I know you're busy—it's right in the middle of recruiting—but I feel like I want to be a football coach. I want to dedicate my life to coaching young men. And I need some advice from a man who's a professional.' Coach Tyler said, 'Excuse me a minute, son.' He picked up the telephone, dialed his secretary, and said, 'Tell everybody who wants to see me that I'd be glad to see them, but they ought to know that I'm going to be tied up here for at least an hour." Then he jumped up. 'Son, congratulations. There isn't anything I'd rather see a young man do than dedicate his life to work with young people and be a coach. Congratulations, Ray, you're so far ahead of me when I was your age. If I would have had guts enough when I was your age to go in and see Coach Vaught at Ole Miss, I believe he would have assisted me and given me encouragement like I'm fixing to give you.' "

Now that's the way to deal with young people.

I don't care how good you can pick a guitar, how good you can sing, how good you can tell a story, how good you can perform . . . if you still ain't good people, you ain't nothing.

13

Friends

We're better than good friends. I look at him as a beloved Christian brother. Jerry's the same tomorrow as he was today.

Jerry is genuine. He's what he purports to be . . . what he says he is. He has that ability to transmute a little base element in the gold. It's like eighteen karat gold. Everybody appreciates something genuine.

OWEN COOPER

A RECORD COMPANY executive asked me if I would talk to one of their young artists who, in the matter of six months, was a superstar. "What do you want me to talk to him about?"

"You ought to know how to talk to him—aren't you the Chaplain of Country Music?"

He told me that the young man thought that to become a star he needed to take a few pills and smoke a little marijuana. I sat the young man down and talked to him in a spirit of love just like he was my own son. When I finished, he shook my hand. "Thank you so much, Mr. Clower."

Since then I've heard this young star being interviewed on radio, and they asked him about some of the people he has met in show business that he likes —and he usually brings up my name. So apparently I did it in such a manner that I wasn't trying to straighten him out or preach to him—I wanted to let him know that I loved him, and, by so loving him, I wanted to share a better way. You don't have to get off on strong drink or pills in order to be a star—that ain't even part of it. I can give you testimony after testimony about some superstars who threw away a few years of their lives fooling with drugs.

One of the greatest blessings God has given me is friends. I've never met an artist who was ugly to me. I've been warned that some of them were a little temperamental or "watch them" or "be careful how you handle this one." I was even told by MCA Records in Hollywood at Universal Studios: "We've signed you. The next thing for you to do is hurry to Nashville and make sure Owen Bradley likes you."

I took the attitude right then that if Owen Bradley liked me, he'd like me the way I was. Folks shouldn't be different things to different folks. I'm Jerry Clower from Rt. 4, Liberty, Mississippi. If I've been successful, it's because I've remained myself and haven't tried to live a lie. I live who I am. And I hasten to say, hallelujah! Mr. Bradley does like me. Beautiful. When I went to Nashville, he took me to lunch at twelve o'clock, and he told his secretary Polly that we would be back in an hour. We got back at four o'clock. He had laughed until both eyes were plum red. And all I was doing was talking to him. I wasn't trying to impress him other than I hoped he would be impressed with the way I was doing.

We went to lunch, and we all just fell in love with Jerry. It's been that way ever since. How are you going to not like him?

OWEN BRADLEY

You'd better watch Jimmy Dean when you're on his show, I was told. Why, Jimmy Dean and I are buddies. He can get in a fist fight over me, and I'd get in a fist fight over him. He has been honest with me. I was the first artist ever to repeat on his show. At the end of the second show, he hugged me and said, "You big funny sonofagun, I love you. But you ain't fixing to take over my TV show. I'll help you get your own, but you ain't going to take over mine." This is beautiful. Maybe I came on a little too strong on some shows —and they didn't have me back. But I think they should have been honest with me. I enjoy doing the national TV talk shows about as much as anything I do.

Connie Smith is another real person. And Tennessee Ernie Ford. It was love at first sight when I met him. We started clowning and he'd call me a peapicker, and I'd do that old country talk to him, and we got to talking about his trip to Russia. I complimented him on hearing him pray at the Martha White Banquet— and how wonderful it was that a guy of his caliber would be called on to pray publicly.

I've been thrilled to do shows with such stars as Merle Haggard, and be a member of the Grand Ole Opry, and meet so many wonderful people there, including the management of the Opry. It's so great to see how a big business like that can be run in such a manner that it's like a big family. I'm sure proud to be a part of it.

Mike Douglas is one of my favorite folks. He's so courteous, so nice. "How are you, Jerry? It's good to see you. I'm so glad to have you on my show."

Ralph Emery and I are dear friends. And T. Tommy Cutrer. And Chic Doherty—in my opinion, the most knowledgeable man in all of the record world on how to sell a record. He came up through the ranks. Let's face it, I'm a pretty good peddler. I was in sales a lot longer than I've been in show business. I'm a professional salesman, and my first love is selling. That's why I enjoy doing so many commercials now. Chic helped me by pushing, and calling, and promoting. He has been married to the same lady for some thirty-odd years, and my wife and his wife could relate and visit. It wasn't like a cold-blooded record executive but like a buddy. When I speak in a church in Nashville as a Christian entertainer, he always comes and brings his wife and his daughter Patsy.

There's David Frost—the greatest interviewer who ever interviewed me. "Jerry, I understand you're a lay preacher—what does that mean?"

"It means I'm not ordained, but I love the Lord as much as the preacher does."

"Isn't it wonderful how God can take a tragic thing or a disability and use that to his glory?"

"Amen, David Frost. But I didn't know you even talked like this."

"Yes, my father was a preacher. And one time my grandmother was traveling in a carriage and it turned over. She fell and turned in midair to protect her baby. She fell on the cobblestone street and slammed with such force that it deafened her. In raising her child—my father—this boy would look into the eyes of his mother and he would enunciate clearly so she could read his lips. And because he had to do this, my father up in the pulpit is now the greatest preacher I've ever heard. He pronounces and enunciates so properly. Why? Because of a disability of his mother. God took that and used it so my father would be a better preacher."

After I did the David Frost show, I went back to do the Mike Douglas show. One of the ushers said, "Mr. Clower, hurry up—there's a guy here running us crazy. He's the biggest fan you've got. The minute you got here he wanted me to bring you to his dressing room." I thought it was Marty Robbins, or Faron Young, or Bill Anderson, or Willie Nelson. I ran and knocked on the dressing room door, and it was David Frost. He's such a great talent. Debbie Reynolds, Nanette Fabray, and Mr. Pierre Cardin were on the Frost show the day I was on. Now can't you see me talking to Pierre

Cardin. He's a little Frenchman. He sews. He makes clothes. He had invented some Pierre Cardin cologne for men, and asked, "Jereee, what do you use for cologne down in Mississippi?"

"Mr. Cardin, we just slosh on whatever our young'-uns give us at Christmas."

Debbie Reynolds laughed and said, "Jerry, what a beautiful line."

"That ain't no beautiful line. That's what I use. Whatever my young'uns get me."

When I was in Hollywood at the Universal Studios commissary, I was telling the MCA record executive that Telly Savalas is my favorite talent as far as raw ability and acting is concerned. About that time he came walking in. "My goodness, on occasion I'm disturbed by folks who want my autograph, especially when I'm eating—it's rough. You can't even eat. But I just got to speak to him because I think he's something." So I walked up to him. "Mr. Savalas—"

"Yes."

"I want ten seconds of your time."

"All right, go ahead."

"I'm Jerry Clower. I work for Music Corporation of America, just like you do. You make TV shows and movies for them, and I make records. I am a country performer. I am in show business. I am a member of the world famous Grand Ole Opry, and I tell country stories. I think you're the greatest talent in the world today. And I just wanted to tell you. Thank you, Mr. Savalas."

I started walking off, and he shouted, "Wait a minute!"

He got up from the table, put his hand on the back of my neck, grabbed it, and got right up in my face —just like he does on television. "You're beautiful," he said. "I hear your records on KLAC—you're a great talent. I dig you."

The MCA folks just went wild. They ran and got a camera. And now there's a 16x24 picture hanging in my den, and it's autographed: "From Telly Savalas to My Buddy Jerry."

Friends have meant so much to me through the years. The five closest personal friends I have in the world are Charles J. Jackson, Chief Carey S. Hill, Alcus Smith, Owen Cooper, and Bill Woodruff, one of my beloved neighbors in Yazoo City. They love me and pray for me. And, of course, one of my dearest, newest, and closest friends is Tandy Rice.

Charles J. Jackson, Mississippi Chemical's vice-president in charge of sales, was my boss when I was a full-time fertilizer salesman. If they were going to shoot one of us, I'd tell them to shoot me, but to make sure that when the bullet hit me that it didn't ricochet and hurt Charles in any way. I don't want anything to happen to him.

After I had been in show business six months, Charles put his arm around me one day and said, "We have a sharing group that meets every so often, and one of the things we do is pray for you. We pray that you won't change. That you will remain the Christian man that you are and have been trying to be."

He's the most free-hearted person I've ever seen. He's making all of this money, but he's not keeping all this money. He'll give it away to the first fellow passing by who looks like he needs it. He'll literally give the shirt off his back. Literally. He's that kind of guy. This contributes as much to any person's happiness as anything you can do— be free-hearted with whatever you have, whether it's good information, or a kind word, or whether it's monetary help . . . anything to help other people in an unselfish manner brings the greatest satisfaction you can get out of life.

The reason Jerry and I are so close as we are is that we have kindred spirits in many ways, except I don't have his money. But I can get any part of it I want any day I want it. Fortunately, I've not had to do that, but if I did need it—and was down and out—he'd be the first man I'd go to because he'd rally the fastest of anybody. He knows the same thing about me.

CHARLES J. JACKSON

After an Opry appearance, a man—who was an acquaintance then, but a friend now—called me backstage. "Don't you ever change," this man—Bill Anderson—told me. "If you change, nobody will ever believe anything about Christian folks again. And don't let anybody change you show-business-wise."

Dinah Shore gave me the same advice. She loves me and I love her. I've got a two-page handwritten letter from Dinah and a picture she sent me hanging on the wall, and I know she's a busy woman. "You're a country comic, Jerry, and you have been accepted everywhere. Your albums have sold everywhere. And the minute you let them change you to try to be something other than what you are, you're probably going to mess up. Some of you Nashville folks and Grand Ole Opry people will get involved in Hollywood and change. Don't change."

My friends have given me valuable advice through the years while I was backing into show business and making the adjustment. I was getting on up in years before anybody ever dared me to make a record. A music executive commented, "Jerry reminds me of a twenty-nine-year-old rookie who just broke into baseball and made the all-star team."

The greatest all-around moral Christian gentleman I've ever known is Owen Cooper. He had the idea for Mississippi Chemical, hired the people, sold the stock, promoted it, and this farmer-owned company became a great success story. Some years back they had a series of meetings of farmers to find out their most prevalent problem. The farmers complained, "We can't buy nitrogen fertilizer," and Mr. Cooper said, "Let's build us a plant." "Aw, Owen, you've got to have millions of dollars."

But he believed farmers could do it, and under his

leadership they did do it. It has gone from a few hundred tons of fertilizer a day to the largest fertilizer company in the Midsouth with annual sales of $145 million. Owen Cooper retired in 1974. When I nominated him for president of the Southern Baptist Convention, the Associated Press reported: "Jerry Clower, nationally known country humorist, avowed during his nomination speech not to be funny. But he was just funny enough to capture all of the rural pastors' votes which happens to be a majority."

Owen Cooper is a maximum Christian. He's got sense that he'll never even have to use. He has compassion. He's one of the reasons I changed from being a bigot to a liberal. Some people who didn't know him hated him—and it's so tragic that anybody would have anything against him because he stands for right and truth and Christianity personified. All of those who criticized him, opposed him, and hated him will one day be trying to tear into where he's at because Owen Cooper is going to end up in heaven and have a great reward. To work for a guy like that, and be able to go counsel with him, has been one of the highlights of my Christian life. I'd come in off the road after selling fertilizer and tell him about running into somebody that I talked to about the Lord. He'd forget about the fertilizer, and just want to hear about the talk: "Well, tell me about it." Oh, beautiful, isn't that great?

Around 1959 when I lived at Brookhaven, Mississippi, someone wanted me to go out and see a car salesman who was an alcoholic. I did—and he had been on a toot and had been drunk for two weeks. The house was dark, so I turned on the hall light. As the light reflected in the bedroom, I saw him lying drunk in the middle of the bed surrounded by empty bottles and beer cans. I wept a little. I woke him up, bathed his face with a wet towel, got him up on the edge of the bed, prayed with him, counseled with him, and told him I loved him.

You're talking to a man who would stay drunk for two weeks at a time. I came home from the army as an alcoholic. Since Jerry came into my life fourteen years ago, we met and kept associating with each other. I was an automobile salesman at that time. Jerry started working with me and we got to be real close friends. We were riding around one afternoon and he told me, "I want you to do me a favor." I said, "Well, if I possibly can, Jerry, I will." He said, "You can." I said, "Okay, what is it?" He said, "I want you to quit drinking." And I did.

Since then I was made sales manager of that business, and later my brother and I purchased it and I now operate it as Smith Brothers Motors.

Jerry Clower is the man who led me back to Christ. I have some brothers that I love, but I will sit down and talk to Jerry about some things I will not talk to my brothers about. He's got a heart as big as my television set. He's the most amazing individual I've ever known and the dearest friend that Alcus Smith has ever had.

ALCUS SMITH

In 1974 I got a phone call at home and it was this man, Alcus Smith, ready to be ordained as a deacon at the First Baptist Church in Brookhaven. And he told them he wouldn't take it unless I came.

So I went and sat in the audience with the lieutenant governor of Mississippi. Alcus got up and told how he had come from the service as an alcoholic and the Lord had sent a young fertilizer salesman to Brookhaven. "I became a Christian at an early age," he explained. "God didn't leave me—I left him. But after meeting Jerry Clower and fellowshiping with him, I came back to the Lord, back to my family. I now own the motor company I used to work for, and I have grown in grace. Tonight I'll be ordained as a deacon in my church."

A beautiful fountain pen and pencil set came through

the mail bearing this card from Alcus: "Thanks to you, I haven't had a drink in so many years. Today is my anniversary. Praise God, I'm glad I am saved." I get Father's Day presents, Christmas presents, gifts of all types, but I've never received a present in all of my life that caused my old heart to beat with joy any more than this gift from Alcus on the anniversary of his re-dedicating his life to Jesus and depending on him to help whip this damnable addiction to alcohol.

I praised God for this, but I deserve no credit. I was doing what any Christian with any kind of compassion ought to do. I believe the Good News, and folks ought to spread it. But I'm very careful to make sure if I get on a big talk show that the word doesn't get out that "You'd better watch ol' Clower—all he'll do is preach." I know people who will walk up to some of us and ask, "What do you think about the weather?" and before we can answer, they've preached a fifteen-minute sermon. I don't think the Lord wants us to do this. It hurts more than it helps.

You have to work up a sweat to talk about Jerry. He's country, he's honest, he's fair, and he's good to everybody.

We fish once in a while and we sit out here in the backyard and talk about things. About back when we were growing up . . . cooking billy-goat and chitlins, going coon hunting, going to the swimming hole, and about the comical people we met when we were growing up. We talk about how we used to ride them mules, ride horses. Man, used to have a time. Plowed them cottonfields, dug them potatoes . . .

Nearly everybody he has met and known has contributed something to Jerry. If he aggravates anybody—or sees that a fellow is offended—he gets away from that person. Jerry and I kind of look down the same fence.

Everywhere we've been together, we had a good time. We made it that way. Jerry never had too much respect for money. If a fellow was broke, he'd give him a few dollars of what he had. His good times was in doing something for people. He loves to preach. This has contributed to what he is now.

I've seen the time when we wouldn't have but a few dollars, we'd go somewhere on Saturday night and come back on Sunday night, and we'd have to dig deep to get up enough money to eat some hamburgers on the way home. We had a tank of gas and we knew we could get home, so we'd get them hamburgers and come on in.

CHIEF CAREY S. HILL

Chief Hill is a man among men. He owns a welding shop in Yazoo City—and our backyards join. I got involved with him as a neighbor and started loving him. At one time he had a drink problem, but I helped him with it by showing him that he can have more fun with me than he can drinking. Don't nobody have more fun than I do. I get it on. I enjoy living. Chief Hill and I get to talking and he brings up some things that remind me of what I did when I was a kid and, consequently, I remember a story that I ought to tell and put it on a record.

Chief Hill doesn't try to be something that he ain't. He came up poor, similar to me. He has worked hard all his life, and he represents the working-class people in this country. This is where it's at. The folks who work with their hands and know what's going on. He wants to do the right thing toward other people, and he has a lot of wisdom in the things he says. He is my Country Consultant. There's nothing I can bring up that's country that he can't discuss. Occasionally he'll get a dressed coon and cook it, and we'll sit in his house and eat a coon. He cooks chitlins. Barbecues a goat. And he's married to a Lebanese woman who can cook fantastic dishes of the old country like kibbie and mischee. So during the week when I'm home, I eat barbecue goat and chitlins and coon with Chief

Hill—a part Cherokee Indian and a whole country boy. And every Sunday I eat kibbie and mischee—so I'm the most exotic eater in all of Yazoo County, living by the Hills.

The reason I know Chief Hill is a close personal friend is that the Bible says, "Greater love hath no man than this—that he lay down his life for a friend." I would gladly die for Chief Hill. I would gladly die for Charles J. Jackson. I would gladly die for Alcus Smith, Owen Cooper, Bill Woodruff or Tandy Rice.

I've got all kinds of friends. A man who ran off and left his wife because she made him wear socks. The man who took his big mule and turning plow, and dug a ditch across the dirt road in front of his house so the drivers would slow down and not run over his roosters. The man on trial for stealing cotton—he had planted one acre and processed seven bales. The district attorney asked him, "How do you account for that?"

"I fertilize heavily," he told the D.A.

Folks don't have many friends. If you've got one, you need to love him and cultivate him. One night at Training Union in church we had a lesson on friendship. A lady said, "This is a good lesson. Friends. I'm glad I've got so many."

"How many have you got?" I asked.

"I reckon I've got a thousand."

"Well, folks, a thousand friends—that's beautiful. How many would you call at two o'clock in the morning and wake them up to get them to help you do something?"

"Oooh, I don't know anybody I'd do that to."

"Lady, you ain't got a friend in the world. Not a single friend to your name."

But I can think of some people like Chief Hill, Charles Jackson, Owen Cooper, Alcus Smith, Bill Woodruff, and Tandy Rice . . . that I just pick up the telephone—I don't care what time of night it is—and I'd call them in a minute without batting an eye. They are friends, and that's what friends are for.

14

Headin' for the High Ground

I LIVE ONE day at a time.

I don't have any worldly ambitions. But I would like to play the part of a Protestant preacher or pastor in a movie, and portray him like 99 44/100 percent of them are.

If you'll notice, the TV shows and movies portray the preacher in the show as a nut—as a full-blood killer in many instances. The guy who reads the Bible the most is the one who takes the knife to cut the throats. I resent this. I do not like it.

I wish I could play the part of a pastor and show in the movie how they counsel and render such a beautiful service to a community. I could play this part. And I've got enough pastor friends who could write down experiences they've had, how they've counseled with folks, and how it turned out. I'd like to make a movie like this very much.

Tandy gets on me all the time about not setting goals. "We want to do this by a certain time . . ." Well, he set a bunch of them. And I just don't pay any attention to them. He gets so aggravated. But I live twenty-four hours at a time.

I see these big long-range planning committees of the such-and-such First Baptist Church. "We're going to have a meeting, and we're going to do this and that." Sometimes I don't believe the Lord even knows they are there. He isn't a bit more paying attention to them than a rabbit because they aren't calling on him. And anytime your zeal runs ahead of your knowledge of what God wants done, you're asking for trouble.

His greatest attribute is that he's a Christian gentleman. He'd be relatively happy under adverse circumstances because I've known him when he had no money and he had no prospects of ever making any money to speak of. He spent like he had money, and he talked like he had money, and he acted like he had money. And, later on, he had money.

He doesn't tell funny stories, he tells stories funny. He's a lot funnier in conversation than he is if he's performing. He's this kind of fellow all the time. It's not something that he has to put on in order to do a performance—it's as natural with him as breathing. He performs all the time he's awake. This is his nature. He was born this way. He will die this way.

CHARLES J. JACKSON

One of these days I'm going to die. I don't want to get put into a position where I dictate to folks after I die. As of today—being as I talk so much about Amite County and though I have lived in Yazoo City for the last twenty years—I feel like they'd bring me back to my beloved Amite County and put me over yonder under those long-leaf pine trees.

Possibly that's what they'll do. This is the place of my birth and this is where it all happened. I feel closer to the soil here than anywhere else.

In the event of my death, and my wife intended to

live in Yazoo City and she said, "I want Jerry buried where we're going to continue to live," it wouldn't bother me a bit in the world. I'll leave that up to mama. As far as me demanding that I be put at a certain place, I think we put too much emphasis on that.

Chief Hill says, "When Jerry Clower dies in this old world, we will all get around him down in his beloved Amite County, Mississippi, and then we'll tote him to that high ground."